American Government: The Case for a Return to Federalism

American Government: The Case for a Return to Federalism

by

Joseph C. Ellers

With a foreword by Congressman Lindsey Graham

1stBooks – Rev. 6/6/00

About the Book

Our nation was founded because the greatest political minds of the time had grown weary of the constant assault on their liberties by a powerful, unresponsive national government. When they threw off the yoke of colonialism, they tried to create a government that could never enslave its people. The system they created was a federalist system which recognized the ultimate power of the individual over the two major levels of government designed to serve their needs--the national and state governments. Over the years, driven largely by good intentions, this system has been almost completely obliterated. Special interest groups have lobbied for more and more social programs--administered by the national government--and this has placed significant power in the hands of a relatively small handful of elected officials and bureaucrats. The situation that exists today is very similar to the situation faced by the patriots that founded our nation. At this point, we are susceptible to almost any law or regulation that the national government might choose to impose upon us--and unlike the past, there is no counterweight of powerful state governments to stand up for our interests. This work traces how this situation came to be and proposes some remedies for righting the wrongs. Federalism is more than a term from the past, it is a real safeguard for the freedoms that our ancestors fought and died for. We owe it another look--before the process moves so far forward it can never be reveresed.

Dedication

The work is dedicated to many people. Senator Strom Thurmond and his staff provided much of the information and insight into the history and activities of our government. Congressman Lindsey O. Graham has also been very helpful--both in his insight into some of the issues and for his encouragement and support. Over the years, I have also had the opportunity to work with many outstanding public servants at all levels of government. These people have confirmed my belief that the problems of our nation can be solved if we return to the system of government envisioned by those that created it--and let these people do their jobs. Finally, I want to thank my family--especially my children--Emily, Anna and Allison--because they have made sacrifices to help me complete this work.

Foreword by Lindsey Graham

As a native South Carolinian growing up just miles from the home of the great defender of states' rights and one of the preeminent statesman of the 19th Century, John C. Calhoun, I was instilled with a healthy respect for the powers given to the states under the Constitution.

It's a respect I carry with me in my job today as a U. S. Representative for the Third Congressional District of South Carolina.

In the Halls of Congress, the issues which are debated today have changed greatly since our country was founded, but the underlying role regarding the power of the states in our federal system of government remains the same. Often times, the debate in Congress breaks down not on Republican versus Democrat, but on those who favor the rights' of the states versus those who favor the federal government.

Education is a prime example.

For the better part of the first two hundred years of our country, the education of children was handled by state and local government. Citizens concerned about their child's education ran for election to the local school board and became members of the PTA.

The curriculum students learned was designed to reflect community standards. The norms and traditions of the community were taught and became part of that school's identity. When a town or community needed a new school, the county and state would issue bonds to pay for construction.

Education of children, from the mortar and concrete used to build the school to the types, times, and number of courses their children would be taught was a function of the state and local government.

Beginning in the late 1970's, that began to change. With the creation of the Department of Education, the federal government would no longer be an observer, but an active participant in the funding and regulation of education. Today, the federal government provides about 8 percent of all funds spent on education, but they account for more than half of all the regulations. In addition there are calls to expand the role of the federal government in this area.

Proposals to institute national standardized tests to judge how schools are performing and even bringing the federal government into the once unthinkable area of constructing local schools are routinely bandied about as a way to improve education.

In other areas we have seen the line between the responsibility of state and local government and the federal government completely eliminated. Once power and control is taken, it's unlikely the federal government will ever relinquish control.

That's why it's so important that those of us in positions of authority remember the constitutional role the states play in our federal system of government.

The Founding Fathers gave the states a prominent position of authority. I only hope that our elected officials today will choose to follow their wise counsel.

#####

Introduction

Since the beginning of our nation, there has been a debate over the roles of the different levels of our government. Sometimes, during a national crises, the balance of power swung to the federal government. Most of the time, however, at least through the first hundred and seventy years of our republic, the balance of power remained in the hands of the state and local officials--those closest to the people.

Beginning with the era of the Great Depression, however, the pendulum swung far to the left and Washington began to be regarded as the place where problems should be solved.

Before we begin the process of understanding what happened, we need to reflect briefly on the differences between the conservative and liberal positions and their impact on our lives.

Based on the way that they ran the national government since the Great Depression, liberals believe all problems can be solved by creating a well-funded national bureaucracy. The underlying belief is that things will get better if everyone is dependent on the federal government. This system of relying on the federal government has produced many consequences; among them: a huge tax burden, over-regulated industries that now flee our country, a loss of a sense of community and alienation from our neighbors, a loss of individual responsibility and a tax system that punishes thrift and productivity. These are not the only problems. Our tax system takes problem-solving dollars out of local communities and transfers them to Washington. This tax system also creates conditions where class warfare is encouraged. Another problem of this transfer has been the creation of a huge national bureaucracy. This bureaucracy is nearly indivisible and has been granted vast rule-making powers.

A critical question faces the American people: Do you really believe that compassion is determined by the number of bureaucrats assigned to deal with a problem?

Conservatives believe that competition is good. When

government provides services, it needs to do so in a competitive arena where it faces some of the issues faced by other service providers.

Conservatism also believes that people should have more say in their own destinies. This does not mean that we have no compassion for those unable to care for themselves, but we seek to empower the vast majority of Americans who chose to pursue happiness in their own way--unfettered by unnecessary rules and regulations.

Conservatism relies on an old-fashioned sense of community. This means that the first people to respond to a person in need in Charleston should be the people in Charleston and not the people in Wyoming--via Washington. Local delivery is the ultimate success story. One of the reasons is that local people have compassion with a purpose--they know the local values and they know the people they are helping.

The government should provide a climate that breeds success for all Americans without attempting to dictate outcomes or stifle the desire to compete. We do not believe that the country can prosper when success and failure is determined by the federal government.

We believe that evidence of failure of the liberal agenda is always in front of the people. Ask citizens to cite a government program that produced the desired result in the desired timeframe at the budgeted cost: in fact many of these programs have been dismal failures. Poverty actually grew during Lyndon Johnson's "War on Poverty."

The other partner in this effort, however, must be state and local leaders who need to act decisively when they see problems. The conservative answer is to reduce the size of the federal government and make it more difficult to grow it back. This process starts with empowered state and local governments.

The federal government should also encourage the growth of public-private partnerships. Billions of dollars are raised and spent through local organizations. Coordination of these efforts with local service agencies could greatly reduce the suffering in our country.

Another conservative initiative is to reform the tax code. We need to drastically alter the way Americans pay their federal taxes so that everyone pays their fair share but healthy habits such as saving are encouraged.

We must also curb the federal bureaucracy. They wield too much power. We need to ensure that no new regulations are enacted without Congressional approval. Further, all regulations should have "sunset" requirements.

There is also a need for "term limits" on appointed office holders. To this end, we support term limits for elected officials as well. No one needs to make a career as a Member of Congress. We need a government of citizen-legislators who demonstrate a proficiency in the real world--then serve a few terms in Congress and move on.

Finally, we encourage more citizen participation in the decision-making process. When people do not get involved, it makes it easier for the special interest groups to dominate the national agenda.

Ultimately, as citizens, we have some tough decisions to make. Do we want more or less control of our lives? Do we want the necessary controls to be administered by people we know or by nameless, faceless bureaucrats controlled by Washington?

And one final question, who do you trust to deliver true and lasting change? Unaccountable bureaucrats or your elected officials? We believe that the answer is clear.

Government can do only so much. The rest is up to us.

CHAPTER ONE

The Foundation of Liberty

The United States of America is a great nation; founded on the concepts of individual freedom and equal opportunities for all of our citizens.

These fundamental beliefs are protected by our Constitution. As such, it deserves our support. More than that, we have a responsibility as citizens to study the development of our Constitution. The history of this document leaves little doubt that our Founding Fathers intended to create a national government to serve the interests of the people within specifically defined limits.

A major concept of the framers was their intention to create a system of government designed to preserve the ultimate power of its citizens by distributing political power between a central government and the states that created it. This system is called federalism.

As a check against the potential consolidation of power by the central government, the framers set specific, well-defined limits on its activities and left the balance of this potential power in the hands of the individual states and the people.

A clear statement of their purpose is contained in the Tenth Amendment to the Constitution which was adopted at the insistence of the states as part of the Bill of Rights. It states that "the powers not delegated to the United States by the Constitution, nor prohibited by it to the States, are reserved to the States respectively, or to the people."

There are many specific powers granted to the national government. Among them are national defense, foreign affairs and interstate commerce. These areas are clearly defined in Article One; Section Eight of the Constitution. The powers specified within the Constitution and subsequent amendments are all of the areas where the national government is lawfully empowered to act.

Over the years, however, the national government has

usurped powers and entered into growing numbers of areas where it has no express authority.

The result of these actions is that the framers' vision of a limited national government with specific, enumerated powers has given way to an expansive, intrusive and virtually omnipotent national government.

The states, once hubs of political activity, have been reduced in significant part to administrative units of the national government.

Despite all of the clear evidence regarding the intentions of the framers, a serious problem exists in our nation. A substantial number of political leaders seek to give the government even greater powers. Today, the vast powers vested in the national government have resulted in weakening individual freedoms and the loss of political power in the states.

If the powers within the Constitution can be expanded or altered by the national government without the consent of the people acting through their state governments, then personal liberties are in danger.

As it was created, the base of political power should flow from the state governments to the national government. When individuals joined together, they made specific grants of power to both our state and national governments.

Ultimately, the people must decide on the limits of those powers.

An Outline of Federalism

The concept of federalism was not a new idea created by the framers of the Constitution. These individuals looked as far back as the 13th Century BC and the Israelites. Several Books in the Old Testament present the record of these early efforts to create systems of shared power, including the Books of Joshua, Judges, Samuel and Ezekiel.

The Greek city-states also experimented with a similar government as early as 280-146 BC with the Achaen League.

The first federal style of government that has survived into modern times is in Switzerland whose Cantons formed their first federation in 1291.

Federalism also existed among some of the first settlers of our country. The Pilgrims organized their New England colonies and even their churches on federalist principles.

From that point, American federalism developed at a relatively rapid pace.

The first governments located on the continent were colonial governments. From the very beginning, they were loosely joined together for trade and mutual protection.

As the parent government of Great Britain began to reduce individual freedoms in the colonies, the colonies began to draw closer together. From the Committees of Correspondence organized to speed up communications came the Articles of Association in 1774 and shortly thereafter, the first Continental Congress.

Under this early national government, the states acted as almost independent nations. They were united for one purpose -- to obtain independence from Great Britain.

The Articles of Confederation were the first organized form of national government. They were proposed in 1777 and finally adopted in 1781. This arrangement was viewed as giving too much power to the states, however, and the Articles proved to be unworkable.

For that reason the Continental Congress adopted a resolution in February of 1787 to revise the Articles to give the national government enough power to function effectively without compromising individual freedoms. This process eventually resulted in the Constitution that was ratified in 1789.

Beginning with the Constitutional Convention, our nation has been involved in a continual struggle between the advocates of a strong, centralized national government and those that favor upholding the federal principles embodied in our Constitution.

Alexander Hamilton and Thomas Jefferson disagreed in President George Washington's Cabinet; Federalists clashed with Republicans during the Administration of President John Adams; and three of our greatest Senators -- John C. Calhoun,

Henry Clay and Daniel Webster debated this question in the Nullification issue during the administration of Andrew Jackson. This argument was also one of the root causes of the American Civil War.

Immediately after the Civil War, our system of federal government began to change. The necessity of recovery caused power to flow to the national government. By the turn of the century, our rapid industrialization called for broader regulations to solve national problems. The Great Depression of the 1930s enabled President Franklin D. Roosevelt to expand the federal government directly into agriculture, industry and social welfare.

By the end of his administration, we had seen the most dramatic change in our government. Initially, the federal government took the power it absolutely had to have; under President Roosevelt, the national government took the power it needed to fight and resolve a great national crisis.

The final stage of this evolution occurred during the administrations of Presidents John F. Kennedy and Lyndon B. Johnson. These leaders asserted that the national government could act in any area where it saw a need -- whether that involvement was predicated on Constitutional authority or not.

This theory of government brought with it a host of intrusive programs that bypassed the state governments and acted directly on local government and the people. This time period also saw the growth of national, rule-making bodies. These agencies have substantial authority but are not directly responsible to the people.

Interwoven with these actions has been the rise of judicial activism. The Supreme Court has vastly expanded the powers of the national government through their powers of constitutional interpretation. Federal judges have used previous decisions to take over state prisons and to dictate the operations of local schools. From a constitutional standpoint, these and like activities are the prerogatives of state government.

This set of circumstances is why the issue of federalism is so important today. All Americans should seek to understand how our system of government was intended to operate; how it actually operates; and the reasons that caused this shift away from a federal government of limited, well-defined powers to one that is virtually limitless in scope.

By understanding the problem, we can all take an active part in the measures needed to correct this imbalance of political power.

The Need for Constitutional Remedies

In their wisdom, the framers of the Constitution created a system of government that was not locked in antiquity.

They gave future generations the mechanism to alter their constitution in any way that they might choose. This process is known as a constitutional amendment. It has been used twenty-six times to alter or add provisions to the Constitution.

The ratification of a constitutional amendment is a deliberately complicated process. First, both houses of Congress must approve the proposed amendment by a two-thirds majority. Then, three-fourths of the states must approve the amendment before it becomes law. (Article Five of the Constitution also enables the states to call for a convention to propose constitutional amendments.)

Constitutional amendments are a better alternative than changes rooted only in current public opinion.

The chapters that follow will trace the beginnings and development of our system of government. They are the basis for faith in our Constitution and for the belief in a strict interpretation of the document. In short, this is an attempt to make a case for federalism -- or more specifically, to attempt to awaken an interest in the importance of this concept to our future.

Our success as a nation is attributable, in substantial part, to our basic governing document, the Constitution; and the strength that is rooted in the will of the people.

Our system of government carries with it a responsibility of citizen participation. Through our elected officials, we have a direct say in political matters that impact upon us; from City Hall, through the State Capital, and directly to Washington, D.C.

This opportunity comes with a tremendous burden. If we do not exercise our right to participate, many of the freedoms that we take for granted may one day disappear.

CHAPTER TWO

THE BEGINNING OF AMERICAN GOVERNMENT

Our system of government has been the result of a gradual evolution. In the early days of our country, each development rested squarely on the shoulders of preceding events. Ideas and theories were put forward; debated by the best minds of the country and either accepted or rejected. For the most part, this evolution has been consistent with the ideas that have gone before. Certain ideas and phrases may be seen in all of the major documents of early American government. These ideas formed a solid foundation for the government that was built upon them.

Colonial Times

America was first settled by individuals seeking freedom. To gain it, they risked their lives and fortunes to cross the Atlantic and settle in an unknown world. By the early 1700s, most of the lands that comprised the original 13 colonies were under the dominion of the English crown. Royal charters were issued -- many of which included phrases and ideas in the English Constitution. For several years, colonists had the same basic freedoms that were shared by all English people.

Wars, conflict and an expanding empire forced the British government to take measures that were more and more repressive as time passed. Many of the basic rights were curtailed or lost. Even more importantly, the colonists began to fear that all of their remaining rights were subject to elimination.

American leaders at first sought accommodation. Emissaries were sent to Britain to negotiate with Parliament. From time to time, small concessions were made. But for the most part, the erosion of rights continued. It was in this climate that American leaders sought ways to justify independence. They found philosophical support from a fellow Englishman, John Locke.

John Locke and his Revolutionary Ideas

More than anyone else, John Locke (1632-1704) influenced the early course of independence. His principle works on political philosophy were <u>Two Treatises of Government</u> published in 1690.

Locke put forward the idea that basic freedoms (and authority) flow from the people to their government.

He said, "To understand political power aright, and derive it from its original, we must consider what state all men are naturally in, and that is a state of perfect freedom to order their actions and dispose of their possessions and persons as they think fit, within the bounds of the law of nature...a state also of equality, wherein all the power and jurisdiction is reciprocal, no one having more than another...and undoubted right to dominion and sovereignty." [1]

Compare this phrase with a quote from the Declaration of Independence, "We hold these truths to be self-evident, that all men are created equal,..." Thomas Jefferson, the author of the Declaration, relied heavily on Locke's theories to develop his own ideas on government.

Locke continued that, "When any number of men have so consented to make one community or government, they are presently incorporated and make one body politic, wherein the majority have a right to act and conclude the rest." And that, "Political power is that power which every man having in the state of nature has given up into the hands of society,...with this express or tacit trust, that it shall be employed for their good and the preservation of their property." [2, 3]

An early example of this concept being adopted by the colonial leaders occurs in the Declaration of the Causes and Necessity of Taking Up Arms, drafted on July 6, 1775. This early call to liberty contained this phrase, "...that government was instituted to promote the welfare of mankind, and ought to be administered for the attainment of that end."

These sentiments were also echoed in the Declaration of Independence when Thomas Jefferson wrote, "...that they are endowed by their creator with certain unalienable Rights, that among these are Life, Liberty and the pursuit of Happiness -- That to secure these rights, governments are instituted among Men, deriving their just powers from the consent of the governed,...".

Probably the most far-reaching idea put forward by Locke was that the governed had the right of rebellion if they were not satisfied with their government.

Locke states emphatically that, "...this power (to govern) has its original only from compact and agreement and the mutual consent of those who make up the community. ...And whosoever in authority exceeds the power given him by the law,...may be opposed as any other man who by force invades the right of another." And he added that, "...rebellion being an opposition, not to persons but authority, which is founded only in the constitutions and laws of government, those, whoever they be, who by force break through and by force justify their violation of them, are truly and properly rebels." [4, 5]

This phrasing, too, is found in the Declaration of Independence, "That whenever any Form of Government becomes destructive of those ends, it is the Right of the People to alter or abolish it, and to institute new Government,..."

Consider, too, as you read these words that Americans considered themselves "good English citizens." Their major complaints centered around unfair taxing policies and restraint of trade. They regarded the English government as their government -- and only after repeated requests for change had fallen on deaf ears did they resort to rebellion and dissolution.

These were the basic thoughts and concepts that led to our revolution. The ideas and philosophy were first expressed by John Locke and adopted by American patriots. These ideas found their way into all the important early documents of our government. These truths are so basic and elemental to our system of government that they need little amplification.

Other Concepts and Writings As a Preamble to the Articles of Confederation.

In addition to the writing of John Locke, other theories of government were established and developed during this time.

One of the early arguments centered around the question of the rights of the states. Even before the Declaration of Independence was drafted, some major statements had been made regarding this question.

In the Preamble and Resolution of the Virginia Convention of May 15, 1776, is the following statement, "Resolved, unanimously, that the Delegates appointed to represent this colony in General Congress be instructed to propose to that respectable body to declare the United Colonies free and independent states..." but "...that the power of forming Government for, and the regulations of the internal concerns of each Colony, be left to the respective Colonial legislatures."

Note that the Virginia Delegation proposed to declare free "states" and that it intended for the local matters to be handled by the colonial legislatures. The Declaration of Independence also highlights this concern, "We, therefore, the Representatives of the United States of America, in General Congress, Assembled appealing to the Supreme Judge of the World for the rectitude of our intentions, do , in the Name, and by Authority of the good People of these Colonies, solemnly publish and declare, That the United Colonies are, and of Right ought to be Free and Independent States;...and that as Free and Independent States, they have full power to levy War, conclude Peace, contract Alliances, establish Commerce, and to do all other Acts and Things which Independent States may of rights do."

Here, is a primary example of the continuity of thought expressed by the founders of our government. They note that the organization is composed of individual states (note the plural), each reserving the right to act as a sovereign body. Here, too, they also stipulate the powers that are granted to their union -- "to levy War, conclude Peace, contract Alliances" -- all of which deal with national defense issues.

And they also introduce the right of the union to "establish Commerce."

All were unanimously adopted and all are a legitimate part of our system of government. These activities were a mutual concern of the colonies long before independence. In declaring their independence, they merely reduced these common goals to writing. As will be explained later, these two issues: national defense and commerce, are the two principal aspects of our national government.

First Government Under the Articles of Confederation
While it is true that there was nominal self-government under the Continental Congress, our first real attempt to establish a national government with specifically-defined powers occurred under the Articles of Confederation. These articles were approved by the Continental Congress on November 15, 1777 -- at the very beginning of the War for Independence. It was not until March 1, 1781 (and Maryland's ratification) that they officially went into effect.

The intentions of the leaders of our government at that time were clear. They created a national government for two main purposes -- to conduct foreign affairs (including national defense) and to coordinate the establishment of international trade. The powers that were given to the national government were strictly limited.

These early Americans had a great love for individual liberties. They perceived powerful central governments as a threat to these freedoms. This dislike of the centralized political power of Great Britain and the colonial aristocracy was one of the primary reasons behind the American Revolution. There can be no question that our first leaders intended to do everything that they could to prevent centralized government from springing up here. [6]

A second reason for limiting national powers was the loyalty that these leaders felt for their particular states. Thomas Jefferson was an American, but he was a Virginian first.[7]

This situation was heightened because the members of the Continental Congress were not elected nationally but as representatives of their individual states. When the Continental Congress drafted the Articles of Confederation, it was their intention to create "a government which left their constituents (the states and the people) in the place of supremacy." [8]

This was part of the early debate. These leaders realized that they had a choice between creating "a sovereign state, or a number of confederated states." [9]

By adopting the Articles of Confederation, they clearly demonstrated their intention to maintain the sovereignty of the individual states. A close look at the Articles of Confederation is warranted. Several key statements clearly show the framework that was intended for national government.

After naming each state as a member of the compact, Article II reads that, "Each state retains its sovereignty, freedom and independence, and every Power, Jurisdiction and right, which is not by this confederation expressly delegated to the United States, in Congress assembled."

Each state was intended to function as a self contained governmental unit.

The union was only for certain specific purposes. As expressed in Article III, "The said states hereby severally enter into a firm league of friendship with each other, for their common defense, the security of their Liberties, and their mutual and general welfare,..."

This was followed by a series of articles that specifically outlined the powers of the national government: to create a treasury, levy taxes, issue and borrow money; to wage war; enter into treaties; regulate trade; manage Indian affairs; establish a postal system; appoint all military officers; and to appropriate funds for defraying public expenses.

Every power stated here was related to foreign affairs. Even the provisions that dealt with raising funds were specifically to fund military forces. It is also notable that the states agreed to abandon some powers and transfer them to the national government. The states agreed not to enter into alliances with foreign governments and with each other without the consent of Congress. They also agreed not to keep warships in times of peace and to maintain only nominal militias.

The only other major area that the Articles of Confederation covered involved the judicial system. Congress was empowered to appoint courts "...for trial of piracies and felonies committed on the high seas" only. The National Congress reserved to itself the right to settle, on appeal, "...all disputes and differences now subsisting or that hereafter may arise between two or more states..." A national judiciary was almost an afterthought and its scope was confined to areas not within the jurisdictions of individual states.

An even more important point is that Congress originally intended for disputes between the states (and by inference, between the states and the national government) to be settled by the people's representatives in Congress. At this stage, there was no intention of creating a powerful judicial branch of the national government or any kind of executive branch at all.

The states intended to continue functioning as they had during the revolution -- as independent entities. In several states, the chief executive was referred to as a President -- rather than as a governor.

When you look back on these events and the system of government that was created under the Articles of Confederation, it is not difficult to understand why this first government was so inoperable, unworkable and weak. Its hands were tied at every turn.

These early leaders had succeeded in creating a national government that was subservient to the state governments. Because of its weaknesses and lack of duties, few competent men agreed to serve and attendance at the Continental Congress began to drop.

The weakness of the national government was called into sharp focus in 1786, when Daniel Shays led a rebellion against Massachusetts. The national government was unable to assist in any way. Massachusetts was left to its own devices to counter the threat.

This, and other similar events, began to convince the leaders of various states that something needed to be done to redress the imbalance of powers in the Articles of Confederation.

Later in 1786, representatives from five states met in Annapolis, Maryland, to propose that a convention be called in Philadelphia for the purpose of revising the Articles of Confederation.

Their hope, and the hope of those that attended the

convention, was to create a system of government that provided for a strong national government with certain well-defined powers; while, at the same time, allowing the states (and thereby the individual) to continue to control the great bulk of governmental decisions.

To do this, they had to create a system that shared powers between two levels of government that served the same citizens. The system that emerged is known as federalism.

CHAPTER THREE

THE CONSTITUTION

The Constitution of the United States is the supreme law of our nation. For over two hundred years, it has been the cornerstone of liberty and has protected us from the enemies of liberty. This protection is the central purpose of the Constitution. Far from being a blueprint for daily operations of our government, a major purpose for its creation was to protect us from the tyranny of an overpowering central authority.

The record of the constitutional debates contains ample evidence to substantiate the claim that its main purpose was not to create a perfect system of government, but to protect its citizens from potential abuses that could occur with other forms of national government. The inclusion of checks and balances and separation of powers are proof that their efforts were aimed at the decentralization of power -- thereby, hopefully preventing its abuse.

Today, many people assert that the Constitution is a "living" document. If by that they intend for its principles to be consistently applied to changing social conditions and technology, then they are absolutely correct. Unfortunately, however, this assertion is often used to justify judicial "rewriting" of the Constitution with the change of political administrations.

This constitution, or any constitution, viewed in this fashion fails its own test -- precisely because it does not provide constant protection against overzealous authority.

Our Constitution was written is such a manner that it allowed future generations to change it. This change is known as a constitutional amendment. Since the beginning of our government, this method has been used twenty-six times.

Although some claim that this process is cumbersome and time-consuming, these were the very safeguards intended by the framers. This safeguard prevents some minor crises from

15

eroding the liberties of those citizens that the Constitution was drafted to protect.

This process is especially important because it ensures that the government closest to the people -- state governments -- must have a say in any major changes. This is consistent with the previous reasoning found in establishing our government.

The procedure for adopting a constitutional amendment and conducting the affairs of our nation was devised during the Constitutional Convention in Philadelphia in 1787. This convention did not deviate in great measure from any of the actions taken in organizing our first government. The words and ideas of John Locke; the ideas contained in the Declaration of Independence; and even some of the ideas of the Articles of Confederation found their way into the Constitution.

This process and the people that were responsible for it are an important part of our history.

The Constitutional Convention

The Constitutional Convention was to open on May 14, 1787, but it was not until May 25 when delegates from a quorum of seven states arrived that the proceedings began. The convention was called for the "sole and express purpose of revising the Articles of Confederation."

As the summer wore on, the delegates abandoned this idea but it was their original intention.

The representation at the convention was governed by the same principles that applied under the Articles of Confederation. Each state, regardless of size, was entitled to one vote. If a state's delegation was evenly divided on a certain question, it had no vote on that issue.

This system of voting reflected the situation in the country at that time -- the states were regarded as completely separate of each other, sovereign, equal and all-powerful; with only the need for common defense as a uniting factor.

Even the ratification process favored the sovereignty of the states. The final document was not to be presented to a national convention of the people or submitted to the Continental

Congress -- instead, the various states were called upon to ratify the document.

The one difference between these requirements and those of the Articles of Confederation was that only nine states had to ratify to implement the new constitution. The Articles had required unanimous assent for adoption and amendments.

This assemblage included most of the prominent political minds of the times. Almost all of those present had been soldiers or administrators during the Revolution. Among them were Benjamin Franklin, the elder statesman of the Revolution, James Madison, Alexander Hamilton, Governeur Morris and Roger Sherman. General George Washington was unanimously elected president of the Convention; and as such took little part in the debates, themselves.

Another handful of patriot leaders were absent; among them John Adams, John Jay, and Thomas Jefferson. Patrick Henry refused to attend because of his opposition to any form of strong national government.

Those who attended, however, brought tremendous intellect and an unrivaled understanding of human nature to the debates. For the most part, they were educated in the style of those days, with tremendous emphasis on history and philosophy. To this was added their knowledge of government as it then existed throughout the world. These arguments were based on principle. Yet, even where they disagreed, all were obviously concerned about the future of the nation and the great experiment known as America.

The debates themselves were conducted in absolute secrecy. They had no intention of allowing a premature disclosure of the events to defeat their efforts before they began.

Even though the debates were not public, several of those present kept notes of the proceedings. The most detailed were kept by James Madison of Virginia. It is here that the best evidence of original intent is to be found.

Basic Conflicts of the Convention

In any gathering of intelligent individuals, many varying

opinions are expected to exist. Unlike our government of today, there were no political parties. As a matter of fact, it was the intention of our leaders to avoid the creation of political parties. The divisions that existed at the convention were at the heart of the eventual creation of political parties and at the time of the convention took three main forms.

The first major area of disagreement -- and the one that prompted the convention was the difference of opinion over where the great bulk of political power should lie. Those that favored a strong central government had Alexander Hamilton of New York as one of their leaders. Those that favored strengthening the national government, but clearly defining its powers -- and leaving most of the power at the state level had advocates such as James Madison of Virginia, Roger Sherman of Connecticut, and Edmund Randolph of Virginia.

In addition to this divergence was the tension between the small states and the three large ones (Massachusetts, Pennsylvania and Virginia). This conflict resulted in the proportional representation in the House of Representatives and equal representation in the Senate. The theory behind this plan (proposed by Roger Sherman) was that the large states would dominate the House and the smaller states would dominate the Senate, and in this way no group would be able to force its will on the other.

Moreover, tension existed between the commercial northern states and the agrarian southern states. This manifested itself in the areas of representation, taxation and trade. These issues were later to divide the Union for a time.

Nevertheless, compromise prevailed at the Constitutional Convention. The goal was Union -- and the framers created one that has stood the test of time.

National Power Versus Federal Power

Very early in the debates, it was suggested that the federal system of government that preserved the rights of the states and the individual should be abandoned in favor of a national government with broad powers.

To this position, William Paterson of New Jersey replied, "The idea of a national Government as contradistinguished from a federal one, never entered into the mind of any of them (the people), and to the public mind we must accommodate ourselves. We have no power to go beyond the federal scheme, and if we had the people are not ripe for any other. We must follow the people."

Later, during the debates, Gunning Bedford, Jr. of Delaware agreed that the national government needed more authority which could be done "...by enlarging the federal powers not annihilating the federal system. This is what the people expect. All agree in the necessity of a more efficient government and why not make such an one; as they desire."

At the heart of this debate, however was the question of the rights and powers of the state governments. Luther Martin used some of John Locke's ideas when he said, "that he considered that the separation from Great Britain placed the 13 states in a state of Nature towards each other; that they would have remained in that state till this time; but for the confederation; that they entered into the confederation on the footing of equality; that they met now to amend it on the same footing;..."

His assertion was that the states held supreme power (that power having derived from their citizens) and that they were meeting not to create a government over themselves but a government to serve them.

The concern of the overwhelming majority of the delegates was that the new national government would not be all-powerful but would have only certain specifically ennumerated powers.

On May 31, very early in the debates, Edmund Randolph stated that he did not have "any intention to give indefinite powers to the national legislature, declaring that he was entirely opposed to such an inroad on the State jurisdictions,..."

Sherman continued these thoughts on June 6th when he outlined the principle objects of the Union:

1. Defense against foreign danger.
2. Against internal disputes and a resort to force (disputes between the states)

3. Treaties with foreign nations
4. Regulating foreign   commerce, and drawing revenue from it.

"These and perhaps a few lesser objects alone rendered a Confederation of the States necessary."

James Madison expanded these thoughts when he added that, "These were certainly important and necessary objects; but he combined with them the necessity of providing more effectually for the security of private rights, and the steady dispensation of Justice."

There were those at the convention who sought greatly expanded national powers.

George Read of Delaware went so far as to suggest that, "Too much attention is betrayed to the State Governments. We must look beyond their continuance.   A national Government must soon of necessity swallow all of them up. They will soon be reduced to the mere office of electing the National Senate (Legislature)."

Read's comments may appear prophetic today, but at the convention it was clear that his views were not shared by a majority.

There are two specific instances in which the framers considered proposals that would allow the national government to control the actions of the state governments. The first of these was proposed by Charles C. Pinckney of South Carolina. On June 8th, he proposed that "the National legislature should have authority to negative (veto) all (state) laws which they should judge to be improper." This proposal failed to pass by a vote total of 3 yes; 7 no and one state equally divided.

On two other occasions, Pinckney proposed similar measures that were defeated on the second attempt and withdrawn on the third. On the third attempt, John Rutledge, a fellow South Carolinean, said, "if nothing else, this alone would damn and ought to damn the Constitution. Will any State ever agree to be bound hand and foot in this manner."

This episode is not often mentioned in debates on the intent of the Constitution because this proposal was not adopted. The fact remains, however, that its rejection is important. In no way did the framers intend to create a national government that interfered in patently local matters.

The only other instance involved the times and manner of holding elections for the House of Representatives and the Senate. On this question, a motion was made by Read that, "regulations in each of the foregoing cases may any time, be made or altered by the legislature of the United States." In his notes, Madison writes that "This was meant to give the National Legislature a power not only to alter the provisions of the States, but to make regulations in case the States should fail or refuse altogether."

This proposal was approved and is included in the Constitution as Article I, Section 4; Paragraph 1.

There are other specific instances where states are prevented from taking certain actions by the Constitution, but there are no other instances where the national government is given the specific power to regulate or interfere with the actions of a state in a purely local matter.

If we look at these two actions as a way to define the minimum and maximum extent to which the federal government is entitled to involve itself in local questions, the matter is very simple. In one instance the framers voted not to allow the national government broad powers over the states and in another they granted Congress a specific power to do so. Obviously, then, the framers were aware of what they were doing -- and decided that the national government should concern itself with national issues and allow the state governments to regulate local issues.

Indeed, on the question of which level of government is to have veto power over the actions of the other, the debates leave a clear picture. Remember that until 1913 and the 17th Amendment, United States Senators were appointed directly by the state governments. Speaking in behalf of equal representation in the Senate, Sherman urged the equality of votes, "not so much as a security for the small States; as for the State Governments which could not be preserved unless they were represented and had a negative (veto) in the General Government."

This is not to suggest that daily actions of the national government should be subjected to review from the state capitals. The complexities of government, the change in the method of electing Senators and the political party system have served to create a different environment than the one that existed in 1787.

The point of this review is to demonstrate that the framers intended a federal system where different levels of government dealt with different issues. The National Government has many ennumerated powers granted to it by the Constitution. Custom and circumstances have added many powers to that list.

Yet, the great residue of powers -- and specifically those that deal with issues not referenced in the Constitution -- are reserved to the state governments and the people themselves (see the 10th Amendment). Much has been done to blur the lines between federal and state authority during the last five decades. The lines do exist, however, and it is our challenge to see that they are kept in focus -- as much as is possible, to assist us in dealing with the issues of the future.

The last comment on this issue is probably the most important. After about a month of debate, Luther Martin succinctly stated the situation that faces us today, "...that the General Government was meant merely to preserve the State Governments not to govern individuals: that its powers ought to be kept within narrow limits; that if too little power was given to it, more might be added, but that if too much, it could never be resumed..."

"The great fault of the existing confederacy is its inactivity. It has never been a complaint against Congress that they governed over much. The complaint has been that they governed too little." James Wilson, delegate of Pennsylvania Saturday, July 14 in Convention.

The Federal Government

The delegates assembled in Philadelphia were well aware that they had to create a national government with sufficient strength to lead effectively. The challenge and overriding concern was to do so while protecting the rights of the people.

As an effort to protect the rights of the people, the framers of the Constitution constructed a government that did not consolidate power in any particular branch of government. They remembered the loss of individual rights that resulted when kings and the aristocracy were vested with unlimited power.

The debate over the powers of the Presidency elicited this statement from James Madison, "if it be essential to the preservation of liberty that the Legislative, Executive and Judiciary powers be separate, it is essential to a maintenance of the separation, that they should be independent of each other." (This idea also has its roots in the writings of John Locke.) From this statement is derived the concept of separation of powers. Most of the debate of the convention centered around the division of powers between the two houses of the legislature and between the Congress and the President.

The plan that they finally arrived at contains a series of compromises designed to achieve their objectives and to eliminate conflicts between the large and small states and the southern and northern states. The House of Representatives was to be elected directly by the people with representation proportional to population. In this way, the states with the largest populations would be able to dominate one House. In the Senate, each state had two votes regardless of size. This provided the small states the ability to protect themselves from total domination by the larger states. Part of this compromise was also a concession to those who favored state control of the national government -- the Senators were to be elected by state government--not directly by the people.

As the framers established the legislative branch, they took care to subdivide its powers even further. Their fear was that a totally united legislative branch could easily dominate the President. For this reason, they put the sole power to originate taxing legislation in the hands of the House of Representatives. In turn, the Senate was given the power to "advise and consent" to treaties and to certain presidential appointments, including those of the federal judiciary.

Since the beginning our government has been oriented toward the legislative branch. Almost all of the delegates had legislative experience. The first American government had consisted of the Continental Congress; with no executive and no real judiciary. The result of this legislative orientation is that the so-called "national" powers are in reality delegated to Congress. While the delegates supported a strong legislative branch, they took care to ensure that the President (Executive Branch) also had certain unassailable powers. First, the execution of the laws that Congress enacted was given to the President. Also, the Revolutionary War had shown that military power is best handled, ultimately, by one individual. Under the Constitution, the President is designated as the Commander in Chief of the armed forces.

The President is also given a check on the Congress through the use of veto powers. The President also has a check on the Judiciary through the use of the appointment power.

The third branch of government is the federal judiciary. The Court's purpose was to uphold the Constitution and apply it in certain specified kinds of cases. (The Court was also given original jurisdiction in some very narrow instances.) To keep its justices above political pressures, Supreme Court Justices have life appointments.

The framers of the Constitution did not give the Supreme Court any specific checks over either the Congress or the President. These powers have evolved over time.

The Constitution and the Supreme Court.

In the Constitution, as with the Articles of Confederation, the Judiciary was almost an afterthought. No significant debates were recorded on its proposed powers. In fact, there are only a handful of comments made by the delegates that were reported.

The feeling of the delegates was that because the Judiciary was to have neither the power of the purse nor the power of the sword, that excesses on its part were not to be feared. Congress has two direct checks on their power: the ability to impeach the Justices and the ability to regulate the method and scope of the federal judiciary's appellate jurisdiction.

An initial statement on the intended powers of the Supreme Court was delivered to the Committee of the Whole on June 19 in a plan presented by Edmund Randolph. Article 13 of this plan stated that, "the jurisdiction of the national judiciary shall extend to cases which respect the collection of the national revenue: impeachments of any national officers: and questions which involve the national peace and harmony."

There was no significant debate at that time.

Debate on the Judiciary resumed almost a month later. On August 6th, a plan was presented by John Rutledge. This committee report suggested that, "the Jurisdiction of the Supreme Court shall extend to all cases arising under laws passed by the legislature of the United States; "including questions involving ambassadors, impeachments, admiralty and maritime jurisdictions; controversies between two or more states; controversies between a state and the citizens of another state; citizens of different states; and any state (or a citizen thereof) and foreign nations."

In addition to these specific powers, it was twice suggested that the Supreme Court share in the revisionary (veto) power of laws passed by Congress. Both times, it was defeated. On this question, one delegate went as far as to say that, "he disapproved of the Doctrine that the judges as expositors of the Constitution should have authority to declare a law void. He thought laws ought to be well and cautiously made, and then to be uncontrollable."

The right of the Supreme Court (and the federal court system) to handle cases involving federal laws was not included directly in the Constitution. This right (known as the right of judicial review) was established by the Supreme Court itself, under Chief Justice John Marshall, in the landmark case of Marbury vs. Madison in 1804. This right of judicial review has been used to expand the authority and scope of the court well beyond the intentions of those that created it.

Another significant aspect of the power of the Supreme Court is the assertion that it has jurisdiction over state laws. This will be discussed in greater detail in Chapter Five, but some preamble is necessary here.

Under Article III, Section Two, the Constitution specifically gave the federal courts jurisdiction over controversies "between a State and citizens of another State". The effect of this provision was to give the Supreme Court jurisdiction over the laws of a given state. In 1792, a suit was brought against Georgia, under this provision, by the executor for the estate of Robert Farquahar, of South Carolina. The suit sought recovery of property confiscated during the American Revolution.

By a 4-1 vote, the Supreme Court upheld the right to sue stating that Georgia had joined "a national government, complete in all its parts, with powers legislative, executive and judiciary and in all those powers extending over the whole nation."

The State of Georgia had refused to participate in the case, contending that the national judiciary had no authority in this matter.

The day after the Supreme Court's decision, a resolution was proposed in Congress that become the Eleventh Amendment. This amendment reads, "The judiciary power of the United States shall not be construed to extend to any suit in law or equity, commenced against one of the United States by citizens of another State, or by citizens or subjects of any foreign state." This was an attempt to ensure that the national judiciary did not deal directly with state laws.

In a debate over the addition of new states, Rufus King moved to add that when Congress established new States there should be a prohibition on the States to interfere in private contracts."

To this Governeur Morris responded that, "This would be going too far...The judiciary power of the United States will be a protection in cases within their jurisdiction; and within the State itself a majority must rule, whatever may be the mischief done among themselves."

King's mostion was defeated -- and this, combined with the later adoption of the Eleventh Amendment, served to protect the rights and powers of the States for the time being.

Ratification, The Federalist Papers and the Bill of Rights

As the summer wore on, the pressure on the delegates to complete their work became greater. Some had to return to their practices and businesses -- and the entire New York delegation (save Alexander Hamilton) left the convention long before its work was done.

By mid-September, most of the major issues had been resolved and the remaining minor points were being ironed out. In the aftermath of so many compromises, very few of the delegates were optimistic. Each had compromised so much for the sake of others that they could find very little to be enthusiastic about.

There remained only one major question -- the same question that faced the convention when it first met. How were the powers to be divided between the national government and the state governments?

As late as September 10, one week before the Constitutional Convention was adjourned, Edmund Randolph expressed his opposition to the Constitution, as drafted, because there were questions on "the want of a more definite boundary between the General and State legislatures -- and between the General and State judiciaries."

Randolph's feeling was that the proposed Constitution should be sent to the States, where they could propose amendments, followed by another general convention. Others felt that this was the best of all possible documents; after all, if no one left completely satisfied -- then there was a great possibility that justice had been done. Three members of the Convention, Elbridge Gerry, George Mason and Luther Martin still refused to sign the document.

The draft constitution was overwhelmingly approved on September 17, 1787 and on that day, submitted to the President of Congress. The Congress submitted the proposed Constitution to the several states on September 28, 1787.

Delaware acted quickly and ratified the Constitution on December 7, 1787. Pennsylvania, New Jersey, Georgia and Connecticut followed suit. In all of these cases, their state conventions simply voted their approval of the Constitution without adding any comments or suggesting any amendments. From there, the process of ratification slowed down to a considerable extent.

On February 6, 1788, Massachusetts ratified the Constitution, with the proviso that it did so on the understanding that all powers not specifically given to the national government were to be retained by the states. Here were the first rumblings for a bill of rights.

Maryland was the next state to ratify. This was followed by South Carolina's ratification; again, with the understanding that the unspecified powers were to be reserved to the states. With New Hampshire's ratification on June 20, 1788, began the agitations for a bill of rights to cover specific items omitted from the Constitution. Their ratification notice contained the first mention of the freedom of religion.

Under the rules laid down by the Constitutional Convention, the approval of nine states would activate the Constitution. New Hampshire's ratification was the ninth. Two important states (Virginia and New York) had failed to ratify, however, and the success of the new government depended on these two states.

Alexander Hamilton of New York was an ardent Federalist -- as the proponents of the Constitution called themselves. He recognized the importance of ratification of his state. For that reason, he sought the cooperation of James Madison and John Jay in a series of articles that have come to be known as The Federalist Papers.

The purpose of these articles was to explain the intentions of the Constitution to the citizens of New York. As such, they are valuable to those that search for the original intentions of the framers. In many instances, though, they go much further than the framers of the Constitution intended.

It also needs to be remembered that these articles were being used to convince people to support the new Constitution -- as such, some of the statements made were not as valid as others. The ultimate source for determining the intentions of the framers is in the previous make-up of the government, the constitutional debates and the Constitution, itself.

On June 27, 1788, Virginia ratified. With their ratification came a draft Bill of Rights. This was the first time a bill of rights was mentioned by name. Shortly afterwards, on July 26, New York followed suit. Included with their ratification was a reiteration of the position of the reserved rights of states and a call for a bill of rights.

North Carolina and Rhode Island were the last two states to ratify the Constitution -- Rhode Island not entering the Union until September 29, 1790. They refused to ratify until steps had been taken to introduce a bill of rights.

Based on these occurrences, the Congress sponsored twelve amendments to the Constitution on March 4, 1789. By December 15, 1791, the states had approved ten of those twelve amendments. These ten amendments are collectively known as "The Bill of Rights." Among them are some of our most basic freedoms: freedom of religion, freedom of speech, freedom of the press, and the right of peaceable assembly.

The states insisted on one provision that applies just to them, as sovereign entities. The tenth amendment, mentioned previously, was designed to ensure that all powers not specifically granted to the national government, nor prohibited to them, would be reserved to the States, or to the people.

This was an important provision. Beginning with the agitations of Massachusetts, a majority of the states had insisted on this statement. It was important then -- and it is relevant today.

Unresolved Questions and Omens For the Future

The Constitution of the United States is the supreme law of our country. Many specific issues are addressed; some were avoided. Though the delegates created a document that has stood the test of time, they realized that there was some flaws.

The most significant, and worst, example of the problems that existed in the Constitution was its failure to eliminate the institution of slavery.

This question was specifically addressed in the constitutional debate, Elseworth was quoted on the subject. When the matter was broached on August 20, he said, "The morality or wisdom of slavery are considerations belonging to the States themselves...the States are the best judges of their particular interest."

His views were shared by a majority of the convention. In fact, the only action taken by the framers was their pledge not to interfere with importation of "such persons as any states now existing shall think proper to admit," prior to 1808. That the framers would allow slavery to continue is certain proof that it was their intention that the States have the utmost say in matters within their borders.

The refusal to deal with this issue was also directly related to the eventual war between the states. For while it was ostensibly fought over slavery, a comment from the constitutional debates highlights the feelings of those present -- and what they believed to be the rights of sovereign States.

In a discussion on another matter, this comment was made: "He must be shortsighted indeed who does not foresee that whenever the Southern States shall be more numerous than the Northern, they can and will hold language that will awe them into justice. If they threaten to separate now in case injury shall be done them, will their threats be less urgent or effectual, when force shall back their demands. Even in the intervening period, there will (be) no point of time at which they will not be able to say, do us justice or we will separate."

This cry was raised again in 1798 with the Virginia and Kentucky Resolutions, again during the Nullification Crisis, and finally resolved during the heartbreak of civil war. Yet, these thoughts were consistent with all those that had preceded them. The Constitution is neither a starting place nor a stopping point. It came about as part of the evolution of the American experiment. Through custom and amendment, some of its meaning has changed -- for the most part (as in the elimination of slavery), these changes have been for the best.

The highest tribute that we can pay our Constitution, and those that wrote it, is the consistent application of its principles. To do otherwise is to forget the lesson of history. If our freedoms become dependent on the whims of any group, they become subject to modification and elimination.

The ultimate power and sovereignty lies with all of us -- part of our duty as Americans is to exercise it.

CHAPTER FOUR

THE FEDERALIST ERA: THE TENSIONS CONTINUE

The ratification of the Constitution ushered in a time known as the Federalist Era. These were the days when the infant national government took its first timid steps.

George Washington began his service as the first president elected under the Constitution in 1789. His first Cabinet was composed of Alexander Hamilton as the Secretary of the Treasury; Thomas Jefferson as the Secretary of State; Henry Knox as the Secretary of War and Edmund Randolph as the Attorney General.

From the very beginning, the Cabinet was evenly divided between the proponents of expanded powers for the national government and those that favored the dual sovereignty of federalism.

Alexander Hamilton became the chief advocate of a strong national government and Secretary Knox often followed his lead. Thomas Jefferson defended the rights of the states and the people against increased central authority. He was ably supported by Attorney General Randolph.

It is important to remember that, as yet, there were no political parties. The debates in the Cabinet and government, as a whole, were generally conducted along philosophical lines. The government was united under the reverence for President Washington.

President Washington's approach to government was slightly different than might have been expected. He was from Virginia, and as such, could have been expected to side with Jefferson on the issue of national powers. The difficulties that he experienced as he conducted the War for Independence, however, had led him to assume a nationalistic stance. He did insist on a balanced approach to the problems of the new nation, and for that reason, Jefferson's opinion was sought and often followed. The fact that President Washington was at pains to keep both Hamilton and Jefferson in the government only served to heighten the tension between them.

After eight years as President, Washington retired to Mount Vernon, leaving the government in the hands of our second President, John Adams. His Presidency was more difficult than that of Washington. The emergence of the two-party system, had resulted in a split executive branch. Adams, an ardent Federalist, had Jefferson, a Democrat-Republican as his Vice President. This divergence created tension in the Federalist-dominated Congress that eventually led to the passage of a series of laws (known as the Alien and Sedition Acts) that are surprising by today's standards.

The Alien and Sedition Acts and the response of the States in the form of the Virginia and Kentucky Resolutions of 1798 are an important chapter in the development of our government.

Another significant act occurred at the close of the Federalist era and serves as a postscript. In 1801, John Marshall became Chief Justice of the Untied States Supreme Court. It was during his tenure that the Supreme Court began to assert its influence over the development of American government.

All of these events are critically important -- and they are a continuation of the argument begun during the Articles of Confederation and continued between Alexander Hamilton and Thomas Jefferson. The fact that the argument continues today is indicative of the strong support that exists for both positions.

Hamilton and Jefferson

There has been no other time in our history when differences between two individuals have had such a far-reaching influence over our country. From their disagreements and outright personality clashes have come many aspects of our government that we take for granted.

Alexander Hamilton was born in the West Indies and came to America as a young man to get his education. He was a soldier in the Revolution -- eventually being promoted to lieutenant colonel and serving as the secretary to General Washington.

After the war, he earned his law degree and represented New York in Congress. He was also an advocate of the business and manufacturing interests in the country. Indeed, in his Report on Manufacturers, he called for protective tariffs, bounties for the establishment of new industries, premiums for the improvement of quality; awards for the encouragement of inventions; and exemption from duty of essential imported raw materials. [1]

These, by themselves, would automatically expand the power of the national government. Hamilton believed that these expanded powers were necessary for several reasons -- the chief being that national security had been jeopardized by a weak and inefficient central government. The Federalist argument was that by strengthening the national government, freedom was protected. [2]

Thomas Jefferson was born and educated in Virginia. He, too, was a lawyer but he had a great affection for farming. In addition to drafting the Declaration of Independence and his service in Congress, Jefferson also had distinguished himself in foreign affairs before joining the Cabinet in 1790.

As a member of the Cabinet, Jefferson became an advocate of "minimal government." He favored preservation of farms and an agrarian lifestyle. He had a great fear of a national debt as a mortgage imposed on one generation by another. Yet, as a stout believer in the people, he was prepared to accept their will even when it was against his better judgement. [3-4]

Initially, Jefferson supported some of Hamilton's ideas. As time passed, he began to regard them less favorably. With every new exposure to Hamilton's "energetic government," Jefferson's fears of centralized authority became greater. [5]

As the conflict continued, Jefferson began to regard Hamilton's ideas as dangerous to democracy. He was concerned that Hamilton's ultimate, hidden goal was the creation of an American monarchy. [6]

When the debate moved out of the halls of government and into the street, Hamilton began to accuse Jefferson of being a gullible visionary -- one who had fallen victim to the radical form of democracy then being pursued in the French Revolution.[7]

The conflict between these two giants was both political and personal. They both sought power and both hoped to succeed President Washington. This underlying motive contributed to the personal nature of some of the attacks. [8]

By 1792, their disagreements had succeeded in splitting the Federalist Party into two separate entities. Those that opposed the policies of the Secretary of the Treasury went under the name Republicans (or Democrat-Republicans) and followed the leadership of Thomas Jefferson and James Madison. Those that remained with Hamilton continued to be called Federalists. [9-10]

Since the foundation of these first political parties, they have been a part of the American way of life. Despite the conflict and the great division of opinion that these men perpetuated, history tells us that they shared one overriding passion -- they loved their country. They both did what they thought was best.

Though they both started from this point, their uneasy truce was shattered early on with Hamilton's advocacy of a national bank. As will be seen, it was an issue that would not die.

The Bank of the United States

On December 14,1790, Hamilton submitted a historic report to Congress. In it, he outlined his plans for a national bank that would serve as the principal depository of government funds; the fiscal agent of the Treasury in its domestic and foreign operations and a central control on the operations of the state banks. [11-12]

On February 9, 1791, the Hamiltonian forces in Congress won overwhelming approval in the House of Representatives and the measure came to President Washington for his signature. [13]

President Washington hesitated to immediately sign the bill, however, because of charges made in Congress that a national bank might be unconstitutional. Instead of immediately signing the bill into law, President Washington decided to ask for the opinion of his Cabinet. He first turned to Attorney General Randolph. Without hesitation, Randolph declared the bank to be unconstitutional. [14]

The President then asked for Jefferson's opinion. In a carefully thought out paper, Jefferson outlined his opposition to the bank. He first attacked the corporate character of the bank. An indefinite corporation, "violated every principle of the great laws governing mortmain, alienage, descents, forfeitures and escheats, distribution and monopoly." Since many states already had these laws in effect, the bank must be above these laws and not subject to their jurisdiction. This was not to be tolerated.

His main objection, and the first major assertion of the limited nature of federal powers, dealt with the Tenth Amendment. He asserted that, a single step taken "beyond the boundaries thus especially drawn around the powers of Congress, is to take possession of a boundless field of power, no longer susceptible of an definition." He continued that, "The Federal Government was the creature of the States, with specific granted powers and no others. In every other field, the States were Sovereign and limited only by the will of their respective peoples." [15]

With these two opinions in hand, President Washington turned to Alexander Hamilton -- the chief proponent of the bank. There was no question that Hamilton would defend the constitutionality of the bank. The questions concerned the arguments that he could devise to justify its creation. [16]

Rather than reply to the specific arguments raised by Jefferson, Hamilton used the principle of broad construction. His assertion was that the clause in the Constitution that allows Congress, "To make all laws which shall be necessary and proper for carrying into execution the foregoing powers," enabled Congress to create a bank. His reasoning was that necessary meant "needful, requisite, incidental, useful or conducive to." And since a bank was necessary for collecting taxes, regulating trade and common defense, it followed that incorporation of the bank was within the powers of Congress." [17]

After receiving Hamilton's opinion, and despite all the evidence that suggested that the bank was, indeed, unconstitutional, President Washington signed the bill and the National Bank became law.

One repercussion that was not foreseen was the power that

this interpretation of the necessary and proper clause put into the hands of the national government. It was directly on Hamilton's opinion and often in his words that John Marshall was later to forge his own interpretation of the powers granted to the national government. That occurred during another bank crises, however. [18]

One bright spot for those that favored limited national powers was the renewed alliance between Jefferson and James Madison. As an author of the Federalist Papers, Madison had helped to sway public opinion in favor of more national power. Now, with the creation of an unconstitutional national bank, Madison began to lose enthusiasm for a strong, centralized government. [19]

Madison's reentry on the side of the Democrat-Republicans had not come too soon. By 1793, Jefferson had resigned his post in the administration out of disgust for the way Hamiltonian policies were being implemented. James Madison became an important part of the resistance to the next major abuse of national power: the Alien and Sedition Acts.

The Alien and Sedition Acts and the State's Response

During the American revolution, one nation went out of its way to befriend the patriots -- monarchist France. By 1787, partly because of their involvement in our war, the French treasury was virtually depleted.

The summoning of a meeting of the Estates General (the French Parliament) for the purpose of raising funds, gave the people of France their opportunity to assert their rights. In 1789, the mobs of Paris stormed the Bastille and the French Revolution began. This revolution, on the other side of the Atlantic, proved to be more divisive to American politics than any plan proposed by Alexander Hamilton. [20]

As early as 1789, some American conservatives had concerns about the course of the French Revolution. In 1793, the French radicals (or Jacobins) began their Reign of Terror. This was a time of anarchy in France when hundreds of upper and middle class French were guillotined. In response, the

Federalist Party began to criticize this revolution as an "outpouring from the depths of society of irreligion, anarchy and massacre." [21]

As the Federalists began to lose their enthusiasm for the Revolution, continuing support came from men such as Thomas Jefferson and the Democrat-Republicans. While they deplored the methods employed, it was their belief that the people must rule.

It was during this time that the Democrat-Republicans were rising to power. In the elections of 1796, John Adams, a Federalist, was elected president. But his Vice President was Thomas Jefferson.

The Federalist leaders saw their political power diminishing as a growing number of immigrants, most with Democrat-Republican leanings, continued to pour into the country.

As part of their attack on the Democrat-Republican Party, the Federalists chose to portray them as Jacobins, that is sympathetic to the French at the expense of their own country.

They also decided that the only way to curb the growing power of their political opposition was to restrict the input of these new citizens and prevent Democrat-Republicans from rallying their forces through newspapers and public speeches.

At that time, America was attempting to pursue a neutral course in world events. The British and French continued to quarrel with each other and American leaders were striving to keep America out of that conflict. Both warring nations were interfering with America's right of free trade; with France as a major aggressor. There was an undeclared naval war with France during the late 1790s. By 1798, most Federalist leaders were certain that outright war would be declared with France in the very near future. [22]

With this as background, it is possible to understand that the United States government would want to take some action to protect itself. The efforts actually undertaken by the Federalist government to suppress jacobinism went far beyond mere protection. Their measures ultimately threatened freedom of speech and freedom of the press. This course of events also demonstrated the danger of unchecked national power. [23]

In June and July of 1798, the Federalist-dominated Congress passed four acts that imposed curbs on freedom of speech and of the press. They were also aimed at curtailing the liberty of foreigners. These laws were the Naturalization Act (June 18); the Act Concerning Aliens (June 27); the Act Respecting Alien Enemies (July 6); and the Act for the Punishment of Certain Crimes -- Sedition Act -- (July 14). [24]

The acts are known collectively as the Alien and Sedition Acts. The Naturalization Act raised the term of probationary residence for an alien from 5 to 14 years. The Alien Enemies Act gave the President the power to arrest or deport any aliens that might give evidence of being enemies of the government. This act stipulated that it was effective only during a declared war. Consequently, it was never enforced. The Alien Act gave similar powers to the President in peacetime. It was never enforced. The Sedition Act, it its final form, imposed heavy fines and imprisonment for individuals found guilty of writing, publishing or speaking anything "false, scandalous and malicious" against the government or any officer of the government. [25]

This law found its way into practice. The Administration (aided by Justice Samuel Chase of the Supreme Court) brought 15 indictments under this act. Ten resulted in conviction and punishment. The offenders were chiefly members of the political opposition. Four of the leading Jeffersonian newspapers were attacked and three of the most prominent Democrat-Republican editors were convicted of violating the law. [26]

Today, we look to the Supreme Court for protection against this kind of abuse of personal freedoms. But at that time, the Justices, all Federalists, gave every indication that they would uphold the laws if they were ever brought before them. [27]

With the National Government intent on this major abuse of its powers, the only manner appropriate to resolve this dispute was to bring the question before the ultimate authority: the Constitution and the States that created it.

When Thomas Jefferson and James Madison took up their pens to protest the abuse of federal power, they relied on the founding principle of our government. That is that the people, organized as states, created the national government and therefore, had ultimate control over its actions. These arguments are found in the Virginia and Kentucky Resolutions of 1798.

The Kentucky Resolution was drafted secretly by Thomas Jefferson and introduced by George Nicolas in the Kentucky House of Representatives on November 10, 1798. In it, Jefferson asserts that, "the several States composing the United States of America, are united on the principles of unlimited government; ... they constituted a General Government for special purposes, delegated to that Government certain definite powers, reserving each State to itself, the residuary mass of right to their own self government; and that whensoever the General Government assumes undelegated powers, its acts are unauthoritative, void, and of no force."

He continued that, "the Government created by this compact was not made the exclusive or final judge of the extent of the powers delegated to itself; since that would make its discretion, and not the Constitution, the measure of its powers; but that as all other cases of compact among parties having no common judge, each party has an equal right to judge for itself, as well of infractions as of the mode and measure of redress."

The Resolution ends with the pleas, "That they (other states) will concur with this Commonwealth in considering the said acts as so palpable against the Constitution...that the co-States recurring to their natural right in cases not made federal, will concur in declaring these acts void and of no force, and will each unite with this Commonwealth in requesting their repeal at the next session of Congress."

On Friday, December 21, 1798, John Taylor of Caroline introduced a resolution, drafted by James Madison, into the House of Delegates of Virginia. This statement began with a declaration that Virginia has "a warm attachment to the Union of the States," but that it is "their duty to watch over and oppose every infraction of those principles which constitute the only basis of the Union."

Virginia, too, asserted that the national government is the result of a compact of the States, and that, "the States who are parties thereto, have the right, and are in duty bound, to interpose for arresting the progress of evil, and for maintaining within their respective limits the authorities, rights and liberties appertaining to them."

In their closing statement, however, they did not go quite as far as Kentucky. Instead, they asked all like-minded states to "declare, as it does hereby declare, that the acts aforesaid, are unconstitutional; and that the necessary and proper measures will be taken by each, for cooperating with this State, in maintaining the Authorities, Rights, and Liberties, reserved to the States respectively, or to the People."

At this point, it is proper to note that these arguments are nothing more than a continuation of the Constitutional debates. The most important point, however, is that Thomas Jefferson, author of the Declaration of Independence, and James Madison, the Father of the Constitution, agreed on several main principles.

The most important of these is that the Constitution is to be given a strict interpretation. In the Kentucky Resolution, Jefferson goes so far as to state that the phrase "necessary and proper, ought not to be so construed as themselves to give unlimited powers."

These men also agreed that the Constitution and not the national government (or even the Supreme Court) was the supreme law of the land. They both agreed that this dispute needed to be settled by the states, themselves. To this end, both men directed their Resolutions. Neither suggested that they had the power to declare a law inoperable within their jurisdictions. Both asserted that the Alien and Sedition Acts were void, but they called on the other states to urge Congress to repeal the laws.

That distinction notwithstanding, John C. Calhoun, the noted statesman and orator from South Carolina, turned to these resolutions for support in the Nullification crises (to be discussed later).

The Alien and Sedition laws, themselves, were not the real issue. Indeed, as has been stated, the Alien Act and the Alien Enemies act were never used. The Sedition Act quietly expired on March 3, 1801 and the Naturalization Act was repealed after Jefferson became President. [28]

The real issue here was the insistence by the national government that it has powers greater than those granted to it by the Constitution. Some of the states vigorously opposed this assertion and the matter died quietly for a time. But the argument continued. One sidelight to this story foreshadowed later events. A Federalist attorney who publicly supported the constitutionality of the Alien and Sedition Acts was later to serve as the Chief Justice of the Supreme Court. His name was John Marshall.

The Early Court and Chief Justice John Marshall

The Supreme Court of the United States today bears little resemblance to the original body. The first Supreme Court had only six justices. These individuals did not have the luxury of holding court in the capital city. Instead, they often rode circuit -- traveling from state to state and holding sessions as needed.

It was suggested, regarding one potential nominee, that his weight made him an unlikely judge as it would be difficult for him to bear the rigors of circuit-riding life. [30]

Furthermore, some of the individuals that served on the high court were not the caliber that we have today. One Justice kept constantly on the run to avoid his creditors -- and actually spent time in jail while serving on the bench. [31]

Even the climate within which the judges worked was different. John Rutledge, of South Carolina, was nominated to serve as the Chief Justice by President Washington just a few scant weeks after he had publicly denounced an administration treaty negotiated by John Jay.

The views that Rutledge expressed were anti-Federalist and for that reason, his nomination was later rejected. In a letter to his wife, Vice President Adams said that, "The Senate have refused their consent to the Nomination of Mr. Rutledge. I hope that Chief Justices at least will learn from this to be cautious how they go to popular Meetings especially unlawful assemblies to

Spout Reflections and opposition to legal Acts of Constitutional Authority..." [32]

Supreme Court Justices also were more involved in areas outside of the Court. In August of 1800, the Aurora, a Philadelphia newspaper, criticized this aspect of the Court. In an editorial, it asked the question,"Are they, or are they not necessary?...Chief Justice Ellsworth is in Paris, Judge Chase,...is displaying electioneering tricks in Maryland, and the Supreme Court of the United States, and those who are looking for justice from it are taking a nap in Philadelphia until Judge Chase shall have concluded his gambols!!" [33]

In just a few months, however, an activist Chief Justice named John Marshall would be appointed by President Adams. A contemporary of Marshall's, Justice Joseph Story described him in this fashion, "...tall, slender, not graceful or imposing, but steady and erect. Black hair, small and twinkling eyes, features in general are harmonious." [34]

Marshall's appointment was somewhat surprising, for he had no previous service as a judge before assuming the office of the highest judgeship in the land. He was a widely regarded attorney, but his chief credentials were his party affiliation -- he was an ardent Federalist. [35]

His service as Chief Justice began on February 4, 1801 -- and he was not without support. Charles Cotesworth Pinckney of South Carolina in a letter to a friend on February 12, said, "...It gave me great pleasure to hear that my friend General Marshall had been appointed chief Justice, I hope that nothing will prevent this acceptance of that office at a time when attempts are making to construe away the Energy of our Constitution, to unnerve our Government, and the overthrow of that system by which we have risen to our present prosperity, it is all important that our supreme Judiciary, should be filled by men of Elevated talents, sound Federal principles, and unshaken firmness..." [36]

Even those who opposed Marshall conceded all of these points. Under his leadership, the Court began to assert its powers. The end result of his actions, however, was to enable the national government to expand its powers to a considerable extent -- often at the expense of the states.

There are two cases handled by the Marshall Court that have had the most far-reaching impact: Marbury v. Madison in 1803 and McCulloch v. Maryland in 1819. The case of Marbury v. Madison has been discussed in great detail in many places, and for that reason, will receive only a brief study here.

The basic facts are these: in 1801, William Marbury was appointed as a justice of the peace for the Washington, DC area by President John Adams. His term of office was to begin during Jefferson's administration, however, and James Madison, the Secretary of State, withheld the appointment.

Marbury asked the Supreme Court to require Madison to grant the appointment under Section 13 of the Judiciary Act of 1789. The Court refused to rule on the Section, however, because it said that the Congress had violated the Constitution when it passed Section 13. This was the first time that an act of Congress had been declared unconstitutional and created the doctrine of judicial review of federal laws.

A second far-reaching case involved the Bank of the United States. The charter for the original bank, opposed vehemently by Jefferson, Madison and others, had expired in 1811. In 1816, Congress had passed an act reauthorizing the Bank, a branch of which was established at Baltimore, Maryland in 1818.

The National Bank was a very divisive force in early America. Various states had their own banks and they viewed the National Bank as competition. For this reason, Maryland imposed a stamp duty (tax) on all of the circulating notes of all banks located in Maryland that were not chartered by the State Legislature. The Maryland Branch of the National Bank refused to pay the tax and its cashier, McCulloch, was sued for it. A judgement was issued against him in the state court and he appealed it, on writ of error, to the Supreme Court. [37]

Those that argued in favor of the National Bank were Charles C. Pinckney of South Carolina, William Wirt and Daniel Webster. In the course of his argument, and consistent with his earlier letter, Pinckney said that, "I have a deep and awful conviction that upon that judgement it will depend mainly whether the Constitution which we live and prosper is to be considered like its precursor (Articles of Confederation),...or whether it is to be viewed as a competent guardian of all that is dear to us as a nation." [38]

Daniel Webster also raised similar arguments, seemingly as a warm-up for the great debate over nullification that would come over a decade later.

It is in reviewing Marshall's opinion, however, that we see a throwback to the earliest days of our Constitutional government. One historian remarked that, "A close observer of Marshall's language cannot fail to remark that much is borrowed from Hamilton." The similarity between Hamilton's first arguments for the bank reappear when Marshall states that, "We admit, as all must admit, that the powers of government are limited,...but we think a sound construction of the Constitution must allow the national legislature that discretion...which will enable that body to perform the high duties assigned to it in the manner most beneficial to the people. Let the end be legitimate, let it be within the scope of the Constitution, and all means which are appropriate, which are plainly adapted to that end, which are not prohibited, but consist with the lettered spirit of the Constitution, are constitutional." [39]

Here, in the space of one paragraph, Marshall sanctioned the practice of loose construction and placed the elastic in the "necessary and proper" clause of the Constitution. A second part of the opinion dealt with the conflict of state and federal laws. On that question, he wrote, "...that the power to tax is the power to destroy;...The question is, in truth, a question of supremacy, and if the right of the States is to tax the means employed by the General Government be conceded, the declaration that the Constitution and the laws made in pursuance thereof shall be the supreme law of the land is empty and unmeaning declaration." [40]

These early days show signs of a struggle to build a solid base necessary for the continued existence of a workable federal system. The federal government certainly needs to be able to carry out its legal functions. For this reason, some of the actions of our early government leaders in regards to seeking greater powers are understandable.

The real issue here is not the need presented -- that of a national bank; without a doubt, our country needs some sort of national banking system.. If one had not been created early, it certainly would have been created later. The problem is one of authority -- did the federal government have the authority (without benefit of a Constitutional Amendment) to create a bank? The Supreme Court said that it did.

The problem with judicial interpretation, specifically as it expanded the powers of the national government, lies with the precendents that are set. In our legal system, every single legal decision can be used as the foundation for a later decision. Once a precedent is established, the courts hesitate to reverse themselves.

This is the real danger in the granting of powers by judicial decree. After a while, the tiny additions to national power lead to unchecked and runaway federal authority. Over the years, the inches have turned into miles.

CHAPTER FIVE

CALHOUN, CLAY, WEBSTER AND NULLIFICATION

For almost two centuries, the United States Senate has exercised a special stewardship over the nation. Its "advise and consent" power with the President over appointments and foreign affairs has always given an extra weight to its proceedings. Many of our most able leaders have served in this body.

In the formative years of our country, the United States Senate was blessed by the presence of many outstanding members including John C. Calhoun of South Carolina, Henry Clay of Kentucky and Daniel Webster of Massachusetts.

There are many similarities between their public careers. All were attorneys who entered national politics at about the same time. They all had extraordinary intelligence and an insight into the minds of their countrymen. To this was added their shared desire to serve our country as its President. A final similarity is that despite their talents and ambitions, none of the three were ever elected to this position.

One issue that brought these three giants into conflict was nullification. In its simplest form, a state (or states) declares a federal law void and inoperable within its jurisdiction; pending a decision on the law's constitutionality by the states, as a whole.

This theory was originated by John C. Calhoun in response to a series of protective tariff laws enacted by the national government. The most outspoken opponent of nullification was Daniel Webster--and resolution of the dispute was brought about by Henry Clay. Other major participants in the nullification debate were Senator Robert Y. Hayne of South Carolina and President Andrew Jackson.

Before the crises was over, there were charges of treason and the threat of secession. Given this set of circumstances, it is a tribute to all of those involved that this conflict never escalated into bloodshed and open rebellion.

The Three Leaders

John C. Calhoun (1782-1850) was one of the most distinguished of the pre-Civil War politicians. An honor graduate from Yale in 1804, he served as a congressman from 1811 through 1817. Here, he was known as a "war hawk" due to his support of the War of 1812. In these early days, he was also somewhat of a nationalist; supporting such causes as a protective tariff and the national bank.

From 1817 through 1825, he served as the Secretary of War. Here, he had dealings with another of the great early American leaders, General Andrew Jackson. In 1824, Calhoun was selected as the Vice Presidential running mate to both John Quincy Adams and Andrew Jackson. As a result of an inconclusive election, Adams was eventually selected as the President by the House of Representatives.

Four years later, Calhoun was again elected Vice President, this time, as the running mate of Andrew Jackson. These two began with the same general ideas -- but as time passed, their differences grew.

Henry Clay (1777-1852) came to be known as the "Great Pacificator" for his valiant efforts to strike compromises between different groups. There is no doubt that his efforts in the Missouri Compromise (1820), the Nullification crisis (1832-33) and later in the Great Compromise of 1850 forestalled the American Civil War.

Clay's public career began in the Kentucky Constitutional Convention in 1801. Shortly thereafter, he filled two Senate vacancies before his election to the United States House of Representatives in 1811. He was elected to the Speakership of that body on the first day of the session. Like Calhoun, he, too, supported the War of 1812, so much so that the war has been referred to as "Mr. Clay's War."

Clay also favored a wide array of nationalistic legislation; such as the tariffs, the national bank and public support of internal improvements (roads, canals, etc.) Of the three Senators, Clay's position was the most consistent through the years.

Of the famous orators that America has produced, Daniel

Webster (1782-1852) was probably the greatest of them all. Until recently, excerpts from his speeches were required learning for all school children.

Webster was born in New Hampshire and graduated from Dartmouth College. He then went to Boston to study law and was admitted to the bar. He first served in Congress as a Federalist representative from New Hampshire from 1813 through 1816. At this time, he was an opponent of the tariff policy and an advocate of the rights of the states. In his early days, Webster contended that the Constitution could not be used to destroy the economy of one section of the country. [1]

In the nullification debate, as a Senator from Massachusetts, Webster took the opposite view.

Background

The root cause of the nullification crisis was the feeling, held by several southern states, that policies being pursued by the national government were unfair -- and unconstitutional. The most offensive of these policies was the national tariff.

One of the initial acts of the 1st Congress (in 1789) was to pass a tariff law. Its purpose was twofold: to raise taxes and to encourage and protect the manufacturing interests. The part of the law dealing with protectionism was immediately attacked by advocates of strict construction of the Constitution. They asserted that the Constitution did not give the national government the power to protect manufacturing. The tariffs were low, however, and because the pain was slight, the protests were, too.

Congress followed up this law by increasing these tariffs some 20% in 1816, then doubling them in 1824.

These actions were capped by the passage of the "Tariff of Abominations" in 1828. This tariff placed high duties on manufactured goods, primarily from Britain. This served to stimulate the growth of industry in the New England and middle states. The south, however, was dependent on the sale of staple crops to Britain. Britain threatened to retaliate and impose higher tariffs on southern crops. A result of the increasing tariff was that the price of cotton fell and the southern economy was driven to the point of disaster. [2]

The first response to these high tariffs was the South Carolina Exposition and Protest, secretly drafted by Calhoun in 1828. In it, he stated that a moderate tariff with incidental protection of industry was acceptable, but that the tariffs then in place were unconstitutional and unfair. He suggested that one remedy was to suspend operation of the law within the state of South Carolina until all of the states could be consulted as to its fairness.

Calhoun's reasoning was that the tariff "...worked unnecessary hardship upon the South, strained the loyalty of those who suffered by it, and in the end must work the destruction of the Union." [3]

This protest was adopted prior to the inauguration of Andrew Jackson. As a fellow southerner, it was hoped that Jackson would recommend something acceptable in the way of tariff reduction. Around this time, Jackson had assured the South Carolinians privately that he meant to "quiet the public mind in regard to the tariff", but he carefully avoided further explanation. [4]

Jackson's first year as President passed without any action on the tariff. Southern leaders then looked to Jackson's first annual message to Congress in hopes that something concrete would be done about this issue. But in his December 8th message in 1829, the President recommended nothing satisfactory to South Carolina. The Southern part of the country came to realize that they would not receive any help from Jackson. [5,6]

The Fight Begins

One side issue that directly contributed to the nullification question was the sale of western lands. The national government owned large blocks of land in the western states. Those states wanted the land to be sold at cheap prices so that settlers would continue to come to their states. Any attempt by the national government to curtail this cheap land policy would be opposed by the western states. [7]

There was already a budding alliance between the southern and the western states. Leaders of both sections thought it possible that there was room for accommodation on the question of the tariff and the question of cheap land. The possibility of combining forces came about as a result of a resolution sponsored by Senator Samuel A. Foot of Connecticut.

His resolution would "inquire into the expediency of limiting for a certain period the sales of the public lands as have heretofore been offered for sale, and are subject to at a minimum price."

The effect of this resolution was to limit the sale of new lands until cheaper, less desirable lands, already passed over by the settlers, could be sold. In effect, it would halt land sales. Seizing the opportunity to forge an alliance, Senator Thomas Hart Benton of Missouri -- one of the States directly effected by the resolution -- rose to his feet to oppose the resolution. He contended that this was a plan to slow down settlement of the west in order to keep labor costs down for "tariff-fostered northern factories." [8]

In turn, Senator Robert Y. Hayne of South Carolina stated that public lands should be sold for a reasonable sum to the states in which they lay. This position was in complete support of the cheap land position of the western states. [9]

Hayne's speech was more effective than Benton's. Benton was a brash, raw-boned westerner. Hayne's speech was conciliatory, without attacking any person or section. [10]

At this point, Hayne was careful to keep the issue of western land sales directly in front of the Senate. He refused to allow any of the collateral issues to be considered. [11]

On January 20th, 1830, Webster (now an advocate of a strong central government) rose and delivered his first reply to Hayne. The purpose of this speech was to provoke Hayne into a debate on the constitutional issue of states' rights. Rather than debate Foot's resolution, Webster's speech took the form of an attack on the South, in general, and South Carolina in particular. [12]

53

To a major extent, this tactic was successful. The debate was carried over until January 25th when Hayne delivered his concluding remarks. He was still courteous, but the example set by Webster needed some response and Hayne gave it.

Hayne also fell directly into the trap set by Webster. He abandoned his debate on Foot's resolution and gave a most forceful address on the doctrine of nullification. Hayne concluded that, "In all efforts that have been made by South Carolina to resist the unconstitutional laws which Congress has extended over them, she has kept steadily in view the preservation of the Union, by the only means she believes it can be preserved -- a firm, manly, and steady resistance against usurpation." [13]

The position taken by Hayne was predicated on the already-proffered Exposition and Protest by Calhoun; which was based on the positions of Jefferson and Madison in the Kentucky and Virginia Resolutions. [14]

Many historical scholars have held this position to be substantiated by the facts. Even the method of constitutional amendment (which relied on state sovereignty) was supposed to act as a check on central authority. [15]

Webster was almost gleeful at the prospect of his reply to this speech. He was so certain that this speech would be of historical significance that he commissioned a newspaper reporter who knew shorthand to come to the Senate so that the speech might be saved verbatim. It is from this speech (known as the Second Reply to Hayne) that some of the great descriptive phrases of our government have come. [16]

In his opening remarks promoting the idea that there is one real government of all the people -- national government, Webster said that, "We look upon the States, not as separated, but as united. We love to dwell on that union, and on the mutual happiness which it has so much promoted..." [17]

Webster also used the constitutional record to support his conclusions, "I turned to their communication (the letter from the framers transmitting the proposed constitution to Congress) and read their very words, "The consolidation of the Union," and expressed my devotion to this sort of consolidation, I said, in terms, that I wished not in the slightest degree to augment the powers of this government; that my object was to preserve, not to enlarge; and that by consolidating the Union I understood no more than the strengthening of the Union, and perpetuating it." [18]

These thoughts, eloquently expressed, carry with them some baggage. Remember that it was a contention of the old Federalist Party (of which Webster was a part) that it was only through a strong central government that freedom could be preserved.

Webster then moved to the main point -- his challenge to the nullification doctrine. He said, "The inherent right in the people to reform their government I do not deny; and they have another right, and that is, to resist unconstitutional laws, without overturning the government. It is no doctrine of mine that unconstitutional laws bind the people. The great question is: Whose prerogative is it to decide the constitutionality or unconstitutionality of the laws? On that the debate hinges." [19]

In answer to his own question, Webster outlined his thoughts on the derivation of power of the government. "The general government and the State governments derive their authority from the same source. Neither can, in relation to the other, be called primary, though one is definite and restricted, and the other general and residuary. The national government possesses those powers which it can be shown the people have conferred upon it, and no more. All the rest belong to the State governments, or to the people themselves." [20]

Webster still held that national government is limited. His assertion was that its power flows directly from the people and not from a compact of the states. In this instance, Webster states that a tariff passed by Congress is constitutional and therefore above the laws or wishes of state governments. He stated that, "One of two things is true; either the laws of the Union are beyond the discretion and beyond the control of the states or else we have no constitution of general government, and are thrust back again to the days of the confederation." [21]

Having outlined his position, he closed his argument by painting the nullification theory as a call to rebellion and a prelude to bloodshed. "Direct collision, therefore, between force and force is the unavoidable result of that remedy for the revision of unconstitutional laws which the gentlemen contends for."

And he added, "Talk about it as we will, these doctrines go the length of revolution." [22]

Webster concluded his remarks with a stirring call, "When my eyes shall be turned to behold, for the last time, the sun in heaven, may I not see him shining on the broken and dishonored fragments of a once glorious Union; on States dissevered, discordant, belligerent; on a land rent with civil feuds, or drenched...in fraternal blood. Let their last feeble and lingering glance, rather behold the gorgeous ensign of the republic...Liberty and Union, now and forever, one and inseparable!" [23]

This call to union and his efforts to paint nullification as divisive to the country carried the day. Webster was the clear winner of the debate. On this occasion one very interested observer, unable to do more because of his duty to preside over the proceedings of the Senate was Vice President Calhoun. Calhoun had formulated the Nullification theory but only as a way to head off other, more violent acts of protest. It gave the States the opportunity to take a midway point between complete submission and open rebellion. [24]

It must have been difficult for Calhoun to hear it categorized as a call to violence when that was exactly what he sought to avoid. At this time, however, he had not openly sided with the nullifiers. So the defense was left to Hayne -- and the opening engagement was lost. The scene of battle shifted back to South Carolina and events there conspired to bring Calhoun off of the back bench and into the leadership of the nullification effort.

The Crisis Continues

Andrew Jackson was the nation's first populist President. As the one leader elected by all of the people, he felt a duty to expand the powers of the office to their fullest extent. President Jackson also was resolute and unforgiving. Any kind of slight, real or imagined, was never forgotten. This combination of traits made ending the tariff crises even more difficult than it needed to have been.

Despite the fact that Calhoun was Jackson's Vice President, the two men had their differences. Jackson could not forget that Calhoun, as Secretary of War, had been his superior in the early 1820s. Jackson also held Calhoun partly responsible for the social snubbing of one of his closest associates.

These two factors combined to place Calhoun outside the inner circle almost from the beginning of Jackson's administration. This feeling was then heightened by Calhoun's involvement in the tariff issue which Jackson saw as a challenge to his leadership. The first public clash between these two occurred at a dinner organized to honor Thomas Jefferson on April 13, 1830. At the conclusion of the speeches, many of them hinting at the tariff and nullification issues, President Jackson offered the following toast: "Our Federal Union - It must be preserved."

Calhoun immediately offered the counter-toast: "The Union - next to our liberty most dear."[25]

At this point, the die was cast. President Jackson had accepted the viewpoint that nullification was the same as rebellion. Calhoun had countered by reminding the President that the only purpose of the Union was to preserve liberty.

The scene of events shifted to South Carolina. Despite the possibility of damaging his own aspirations, Calhoun began to contemplate accepting the leadership of the nullification movement.

The responsible elements of South Carolina government had already adopted nullification as the solution. They shared Calhoun's feeling that nullification was a way to prevent violence (or outright secession) and preserve the Union. [26]

In a letter to an associate in 1830, Calhoun states "that if civil discord, revolution, or disunion would follow from the measures contemplated (nullification), I would not hesitate...to throw myself in the current with the view to arrest it at any hazard, but believing that the State,...is acting with devoted loyalty to the Union, no earthly consideration would induce me

to do an act,...which would cast an imputation on her motives..."
[27]

In the summer of 1831, Calhoun came back to his plantation in South Carolina named Fort Hill. Here, he turned his entire focus to the question of nullification. His views were put forth when he made his Fort Hill Address on July 26, 1831. In this address, Calhoun reiterated the case for nullification. He also added some historical explanation.

He stated that the Constitution was a compact between the states that delegated certain powers to the national government. He further stated that those states must have the right to judge the actions of their agent (the national government). If not, then the states had submitted their liberty and their lives to an entity over which they had no control. The obvious solution was for one of the parties to the compact (a state) to interpose to halt the operation of any unconstitutional law.

The national government could then appeal to the ultimate constitution-making power: the states, with the will of 3/4 being final. [28]

The strength of the Fort Hill Address is evidenced by a letter from Daniel Webster to an associate later that fall. In it, he said that Calhoun had recently published the "ablest and most plausible, and therefore the most dangerous vindication of that form of revolution, yet done." [29]

Calhoun had now publicly placed himself at the head of the nullification movement. He did so with the understanding that his presidential ambitions would be ended by this act. These ambitions were secondary to the love he had for his state and for his country.

The next year, 1832, saw an escalation of the crisis. On July 14, President Jackson signed the bill authorizing the Tariff of 1832. This tariff was a continuation of the same protectionist policies with no relief for southern agriculturalists. This time, South Carolina's patience had expired.

In the South Carolina state elections of 1832, the Nullifiers won an overwhelming victory. James Hamilton, Jr., the Governor, called for a special session of the legislature. On

October 25, the South Carolina House and Senate called for a state convention of the people. [30-31]

The decision to allow the people of the state and not just state government to declare the tariffs void was predicated on the views of John Locke -- the people have ultimate sovereignty. Therefore, it would be the people of South Carolina that made the decision and not their state government. The convention was held on November 19, with all of the state leaders (but not Vice President Calhoun) in attendance. [32]

A committee of that convention drafted an ordinance of nullification that was approved on November 24. The ordinance declared the tariffs of 1828/1832 null and void and forbade collection of them within the state. The ordinance stated that no appeal would be allowed to the United States Supreme Court. Further, an oath was prescribed for all civil and military officers of the state and it was proclaimed that any use of force by the federal government would be viewed as dissolving the Union. [33]

The State Legislature then passed all the laws necessary to put the Ordinance of Nullification into effect. Other efforts were underway, as well. On December 26, 1832 detailed instructions were issued for the mobilization of the state militia. Senator Robert Y. Hayne had resigned his Senate seat and returned to South Carolina to serve as its governor, mainly because of his military knowledge. Even as these preparations continued, Governor Hayne continued to insist that South Carolina did not want disunion. [34]

The resignation of Senator Hayne created a vacancy that was filled by Calhoun. After hearing that he had been elected to the seat, Calhoun resigned as Vice President.

The Crises is Resolved

In early December, soon after the news from South Carolina had reached him, President Jackson made two public statements directed towards the tariff/nullification issue. On December 4, he noted that the national debt had been paid and this would enable the federal government to reduce the revenue it had to collect. He hoped that this would "remove those burdens which shall be found to fall unequally" on any one part of the country. This was a reference to reducing the tariff. He ended his message, however, with a warning that the actions of South Carolina would be subject to challenge. [35]

A few days later, he followed up this message with one directed to the Nullifiers. In short, the Proclamation declared that the national government was indivisible; that no state could refuse to obey the law; and that no state could leave the Union, even if it wished to do so.

This proclamation closed with a message directly to the people of South Carolina. The President declared that they were being led to the brink of rebellion and that those efforts would result in the entire might of the federal government being used to enforce the law. [36]

On January 15, 1833, President Jackson asked Congress for the authority to act against South Carolina if the need arose. According to the message, South Carolina was "in the attitude of hostile preparation" and prepared for "military violence." [37]

This request was opposed by Senator Calhoun. In its place, Calhoun substituted three resolutions challenging the constitutionality of the request. He said that there was a clear choice between a "bond of union for mutual advantages, and to be preserved by the concurrent consent of the parts; or a government of the sword." [38]

This courageous stand was made even more so by the threats made against Mr. Calhoun. When he arrived in Washington, there were rumors that he was to be arrested for treason - - and possibly hanged.

On January 28, the Judiciary Committee of the Senate reported a law that gave President Jackson the power that he requested. This law came to be know as the Force Bill.

At this point, the "Great Pacificator" Henry Clay became involved. Even at this early date, Clay was already looked upon as one to whom all the contending parties could turn. In a speech at Martinsburg, VA, Charles J. Faulkner, Esq. said, "...There is one man, and one man only who can save this Union. That man is Henry Clay. I know he has the power -- I believe he will be found to have the patriotism and firmness equal to the occasion." [39]

On February 11, Clay rose and asked permission to introduce legislation that would reduce the tariffs. In that speech, he said, "I behold all around me evidences of the most gratifying prosperity, a prospect which would seem to be without a cloud upon it, were it not that through all parts of the country there exist great dissensions and unhappy distinctions, which, if they can possibly be relieved and reconciled by any broad scheme of legislation adapted to all interests, and regarding the feelings of all sections, ought to be quieted;..." [40]

The compromise tariff that he introduced called for a gradual reduction of tariffs until they stood at the 20% level by 1842, where they were to remain. During the introduction of the bill, he stated that, "I propose to give protection to our manufactured articles, adequate protection for a length of time,...securing the stability of legislation, and allowing for a gradual reduction, on one side: and on the other, proposing to reduce the duties to that revenue standard, for which the opponents of the system have so long contended." [41]

These two bills, the Force Bill and the tariff reduction bill moved side-by-side through the Senate. When the tariff bill was debated on February 25, Webster argued against it and Clay answered him. By March 1st, both bills had passed the Senate and the House of Representatives. President Jackson signed both bills the following day. [42-43]

In South Carolina, the Nullification Ordinance was repealed by another convention. This same convention also passed an ordinance nullifying the Force Bill and then adjourned. These actions, notwithstanding, the crises was over. The hated tariffs were being reduced (with the understanding that the protectionist theories behind them were also repudiated) and the constitutional crisis was over -- for a while.

Conclusion

Advocates of the rights of states have a difficult time dealing with this issue. On the one hand, it can be said that the nullification issue forced the nation to respect the wishes of the minority. There is also no question that in formulating the nullification issue, Calhoun based his theory on the events of history (particularly the Kentucky and Virginia Resolutions).

Upon application, this theory fails. Despite the fact that this country was founded as a compact between various states, the basic theory of majority rule must prevail. Even though these tariffs were damaging to the economy of the South, they were approved by a majority of both houses of Congress (with the Senate still tied closely to the state governments that they represented).

Tariffs are constitutional. Article 1; Section 8, Paragraph One clearly gives Congress the power to impose them. Even Calhoun conceded that nominal protection was acceptable. The real issue here was the degree of protection.

Acceptance of this right of any state to question the degree of a constitutional act of the national government would have resulted in a situation where every act of Congress would be subject to nullification by the states. It is unfortunate that the national government chose to enact these laws which placed a severe hardship on the southern economy. The response that was forthcoming was understandable, given the circumstances.

The greatest misfortune that resulted from this occurrence was the failure of all concerned to comprehend the growing feeling in the South. This sequence of events foreshadowed the War between the States. The national government had demonstrated that it could pass laws detrimental to the interests of the South; that it would do so whenever it felt the need; and, as demonstrated by the Force Bill, that it would enforce these laws at whatever cost. The southernors looked down the road to a continued lessening of the autonomy.

The insistence on protective tariffs by the national government had shown the southern leaders that the rights of the states were diminishing with time. Before long, the South was to reassert its right to state sovereignty and then its right to withdraw from the Union. A second American confederacy would be established -- the Confederate States of America.

CHAPTER SIX

THE CIVIL WAR, THE COMMERCE CLAUSE, AND THE PRELUDE TO THE GREAT DEPRESSION

From December 20, 1860, until General Robert E. Lee's surrender on April 9, 1865, our nation was divided by civil war.

There are many reasons why the war was fought. At its root was the issue of state's rights. Southern leaders were certain that the national government had no regard for their interests (particularly the economic interests of the South).

Southern leaders reached the conclusion that the time had come to reassert their right to control the affairs most basic to the economies of their states.

As the tension escalated, some southerners of strong opinion began to use the earlier arguments of Jefferson, Madison, and Calhoun to suggest that secession was an option open to any state that disagreed with national policy.

This was a gross misrepresentation of the positions of these men. Unfortunately, it was a logical progression of the early arguments and was quickly adopted by the more aggressive elements of the South.

President Abraham Lincoln argued against this position in his First Inaugural Address when he said, "...if destruction of the Union by one or by a part only of the states be lawfully possible, the Union is less perfect than before the Constitution, having lost the vital element of perpetuity. It follows from these views that no state, upon its mere motion, can lawfully get out of the Union -- that resolves and ordinances to that effect are legally void; and that acts of violence within any state or states against the authority of the United States are insurrectionary, or revolutionary, according to circumstances."

An underlying principle of those that favor a strict construction of the Constitution is that the Constitution (and the Union, itself) was created by the states. Some argued that parties to this type of arrangement may have the right to withdraw from that compact -- but there has never been sufficient justification for this belief. This issue was settled, by force, with the victory of the National Government in the Civil War.

The United States Supreme Court expressed its views on the strength of the Union in 1869 with their Texas V. White decision. The basic question before the Supreme Court was, "Had the State of Texas ever left the Union (as a result of the Civil War)?" In the majority opinion, Justice Salmon P. Chase wrote that, "The Constitution, in all its provisions, looks to an indestructible union, composed of indestructible states."

The Court's opinion was clear: the Union, once created cannot be destroyed by any state or group of states. Texas had never left the Union. The Civil War also had a major impact on another aspect of federalism -- the powers of the Federal Government.

The Civil War was the greatest crisis to confront our government. Of necessity, much power was concentrated in the hands of President Lincoln and the Congress. As it would in later years, a national crisis had tipped the scales in favor of a strong, central government.

The Civil War era is in direct contrast to the years preceding it. Despite the early efforts of Hamilton and Marshall, the Federal Government remained relatively weak until the Civil War. Most new government functions were handled by state government. The National Government seemed content to act as a caretaker for the interests of the states. [1]

With the war effort, however, the National Government moved quickly to gain control over currency and banking which had been basically delegated to the states since the 1830s. The military needs of the government also led to active involvement by the national government in railroad construction and operation. This involvement continued long after the need ceased to exist. [2]

The Civil War had other far-reaching ramifications. Three Constitutional Amendments were adopted at the end of the Civil War. Collectively, these are known as the Civil War Amendments.

The 13th Amendment, proclaimed on December 18, 1865, brought an end to slavery. The 15th Amendment, proclaimed on

March 30, 1870, guaranteed that "The right of citizens of the United States to vote shall not be denied on account of race, color, or previous condition of servitude."

This amendment was aimed at former slaves and was essential in ensuring that more of our citizens had the right to participate in our government through the electoral process. The third Civil War Amendment, the 14th, has been the cause of considerable controversy. Proclaimed on July 28, 1868, it states that no "...State (shall) deprive any person of life, liberty, of property, without due process of law; nor deny to any person within its jurisdiction the equal protection of the laws."

This amendment was in direct response to the actions taken by some Southern states that continued to deny African Americans the same rights and protections as those held by other citizens. As intended, this amendment was necessary and proper.

Soon after its enactment, however, actions taken by the Supreme Court and Congress changed and enlarged the scope of this amendment to the point where it is now applied in cases that have little to do with its original intent.

The Fourteenth Amendment and Inactive Government

It is difficult to understand how the narrow Fourteenth Amendment could be so misunderstood.

Ironically, it initially was used to prevent government from acting in many of the areas that it takes for granted today.

Very early in its judicial life, the Fourteenth Amendment was interpreted by the Supreme Court as a check against government involvement in daily matters. Both the states and the national government were prohibited from infringing on major areas of economic and social life. [3]

One national panel defined the situation in this way, "By the first decade of the 20th Century, the "meaning" of the Fourteenth Amendment had been well (if to many minds, incorrectly) established. Certainly, its interpretation had effectuated a new use of the centuries old concept of due process, a new Constitutional "personhood" for corporations, and, indirectly a new and vast source of power for the federal judiciary -- one which was used to assert national supremacy not for its own sake, but for the sake of business. To those "great laboratories of social, political, and economic experimentation" -- the states -- the new national judicial power meant legislative uncertainty and political limitation." [4]

The Rise of Big Business and Federalism

After the Civil War and Reconstruction, the country entered into a time when a major emphasis was on commerce. As a nation, we had been fortunate to have a tremendous source of natural resources. Immigrants were flocking to our shores to take advantage of the opportunities here. These people helped to run our factories and they were motivated to succeed. Men like Andrew Carnegie, John D. Rockefeller and Cornelius Vanderbilt recognized the potential and built huge financial empires.

This tremendous growth might not have been possible without the protections given to our fledgling industries by the Fourteenth Amendment. The twilight zone between state and federal regulations gave rise to significant problems, however.

The prevailing theory in business at that time was that bigger is always better. Power began to centralize among a few individuals using trusts and interlocking directorships of their corporations. In a short period of time, many of our major industries (steel, railroads, minerals) became monopolies.

The states had an interest in controlling these potential problems -- but the Fourteenth Amendment prohibited their intervention. Yet something had to be done. To stem the rising tide of citizen protests, the national government turned to a short phrase in the Constitution to justify their intentions to act in these areas -- the Commerce Clause.

The Commerce Clause

Article 1; Section 8; Subsection Three of the Constitution gives Congress the power to "regulate commerce...among the several states." The intention of the framers of the Constitution was to allow the national government the power to ensure free movement of goods from one state to another.

The original meaning of the Commerce Clause was significantly expanded when the federal government was faced with a need to regulate the railroads.

Several western states had complained about railroad abuses -- particularly unfair pricing practices. In 1886, the United States Supreme Court (based on the 14th Amendment) ruled that the states could not regulate interstate commerce.

In response to this ruling (and predicated on the Commerce Clause), the Congress passed (and the Supreme Court approved) the Interstate Commerce Act in 1887, principally to govern the business affairs of the railroads.

From its beginnings with the Interstate Commerce Act, the Congress began passing more and more legislation that dealt with the railroads. The first follow-up was the Elkins Act (passed in 1903) that prevented rebates from the railroads to preferred customers. Then, the Hepburn Act was passed in 1906 to broaden the regulatory powers of the Interstate Commerce Act. In 1916, the Adamson Act began regulating the wages and hours of railroad employees.

It is apparent from these examples that complaints regarding unfair pricing escalated over a very short time and resulted in regulation of almost every facet of the railroad industry by the national government. The railroads were not alone in attracting Congressional attention.

In 1890, during the administration of President Benjamin Harrison, the Sherman Antitrust Act was passed. This act, again using the Commerce Clause as an umbrella, sought to prohibit huge business conglomerations that restricted interstate trade. Though initially ineffective, it suggested that further encroachments into uncharted areas by the Federal government were possible.

There is no question that action was needed in many of these areas. The only real issue is the fact that all of these additional powers were conferred on the national government not by the will of the people -- speaking through the Constitutional process -- but by the federal courts who allowed this expansion with their rulings on the Commerce Clause. With this framework established, it was only a matter of time before these initial incursions would begin to become the rule and not the exception. It began in 1901 with the Presidency of Theodore Roosevelt.

Theodore Roosevelt and the New Nationalism

Oddly enough, history has not seen fit to attribute the first real expansion of federal powers of the Nineteenth Century to Theodore Roosevelt. Yet, under his leadership, the federal government began the pattern of expanding into areas previously safeguarded against national involvement by the Constitution.

Theodore Roosevelt was elected as the Vice President of William McKinley. Upon McKinley's assassination, Roosevelt occupied the Oval Office and began almost two terms of "reform."

He made his fight against the monopolies and trusts that continued to exist despite the Interstate Commerce and Sherman Antitrust Acts. At his urging, the federal government instigated 44 antitrust actions.

Also at his urging, the Congress established the Department of Commerce and Labor with a Bureau of Corporations. His efforts supported the passage of the Pure Food and Drug Acts and Meat Inspection Act of 1906.

All of these actions were essential, but again the question remains: Would it not have been better to allow the states to regulate the food produced within their borders? President Theodore Roosevelt did not think so.

In most instances, President Roosevelt is best remembered for his "Square Deal." Yet, he had another set of ideals that he considered vitally important. This set of principles was called New Nationalism and Roosevelt felt so strongly about it that he toured the country in 1910 (after his terms had ended) to promote them. Quotes from these speeches sound a great deal like those of his cousin, future President Franklin Delano Roosevelt.

In a speech on August 29, 1910 called "The Nation and the States," Roosevelt deals with the lack of government control and urges sweeping changes:

"The legislative and executive officers of our country,...above all, the judicial officers, are to blame for the fact that there has grown up a neutral land -- a borderland -- in the spheres of action of the national and the state governments -- a borderland over which each government tends to claim that it has the power, and as to which the action of the courts unfortunately has usually been to deny the power to both." [5]

He goes on to suggest that, "...we as a nation should see to it that the people, through their several legislatures, national and state, have complete power of control in all matters that affect the public interest. There should be no means by which any man or group of men could escape the exercise of that control." [6]

Perhaps it is not entirely clear from that passage that President Roosevelt recommended government control of these activities. He cleared that point up the following day in a speech entitled, "The New Nationalism." In it, he said that, "It has been entirely clear that we must have government supervision of the capitalization, not only of public service corporations, including particularly, railways, but of all corporations doing an interstate business." [7]

He added that, "The way out lies, not in attempting to prevent such combinations, but in completely controlling them in the interest of public welfare." [8]

In the same speech, he broadens his call for federal involvement by stating, "We need workmen's compensation acts, both state and national laws to regulate child labor and work for women,..." and he adds a Locke-Jefferson phrase from the past, "The object of government is the welfare of the people." [9-10]

President Roosevelt's understanding of the purpose of our government was markedly different from that originally created by the framers of our Constitution. They plainly and purposefully created a government that would protect its citizens by preventing centralization of power at the national level.

President Roosevelt felt that the national government could take on additional powers without the consent of the people --if it perceived the need. In short, he espoused the belief that more government and centralized authority are the answer to the problems facing our nation.

The negative aspects of this philosophy are evident in many areas:

1) additional government activity requires greater expenditures and higher taxes;

2) every additional power assumed by the national government has been lost somewhere else (the people and the states); and

3) the resulting attitude that the only solutions to our problems come as a result of increasing involvement by the national government.

Big government was supposed to substitute for self-reliance as a remedy for the ills of our nation.

President Theodore Roosevelt introduced this concept to our nation -- his relative, President Franklin D. Roosevelt, made it the centerpiece of national government during the greatest economic crisis in our history -- the Great Depression.

CHAPTER SEVEN

FDR AND THE WELFARE STATE

Of all Presidents, Franklin Delano Roosevelt has aPirguably had the greatest impact on our system of government. One commentary on his Presidency summed up the following consequences of his New Deal policies: permanent enlargement of the power of national government; permanent alteration in the American people's expectations regarding the federal government's role in the economic system of the country; and an end to the doctrine of dual sovereignty. [1]

While there is room to dispute the end of dual sovereignty, the first two issues must be conceded. There has never been a time when the federal government entered into so many areas. In comparison with Roosevelt's presidency, the previous usurpations of power were relatively minor.

Prior to that time, many people had an attitude of self-reliance. Even in 1931, when the Great Depression was tightening its clutches, a good many political leaders felt that the responsibility to bring America back lay with the people and state government. Vermont's Governor Stanley G. Wilson stated that, "I think I am speaking for a great majority of the people of Vermont when I say...that the people of Vermont are for a government supported by the people rather than a people supported by the government." [2]

What caused our nation's policy-makers to change their basic feeling about federal authority? How did we come to look to the federal government for the relief of almost all of society's ills? Insight into the answers to these questions lies with the Great Depression.

The Great Depression

During the 1920s, America knew an unrivaled prosperity. When Herbert Hoover was elected President in 1928, the future looked bright. Unfortunately for both Hoover and the nation, he was faced with the stock market crash of October 29, 1929, and the resulting economic depression.

The initial effects of the Great Depression were disastrous. By the end of 1930, some 6,000,000 Americans were out of work -- that figure rose to 12,000,000 by the end of 1931. During the same time period, there were some 32,000 bankruptcies and 5,000 bank failures.

From all sides, there arose anguished cries for quick action to save the nation from economic despair. Slowly, the Hoover Administration began to involve the national government in efforts to rescue the economy.

President Hoover began a construction program that was designed to improve the country's roads, airports and public buildings. Hoover also created the Reconstruction Finance Corporation and provided two billion dollars (in loans) to assist the banks, industry and the especially hard-pressed farmer.

His efforts were too little, too late however. Many Americans believed that major changes were needed. In the election of 1932, President Hoover was defeated by a man of action.

Franklin D. Roosevelt

Born January 30, 1882, in Hyde Park, New York, Roosevelt had a lengthy career in public service before his election as President. At the age of 29, Roosevelt was elected as state senator in New York.

In the 1912 Presidential elections, Roosevelt supported Woodrow Wilson over his cousin (Teddy Roosevelt). Wilson rewarded this support by naming FDR as an Assistant Secretary of the Navy.

He ran unsuccessfully for the United States Senate from New York and in 1920 he was James M. Cox's Vice Presidential running mate in their unsuccessful attempt to defeat Warren G. Harding and Calvin Coolidge. After the elections in 1920, Roosevelt accepted a position as a bank vice president and awaited his return to politics.

This return was brought about by his involvement in the

campaign of Alfred E. Smith for President. When Smith had secured the nomination in 1928, he asked Roosevelt to run for Governor of New York -- hoping that it would help his own chances. Roosevelt was successful -- Smith was not.

As the Governor of New York, Roosevelt pushed the same kinds of programs that he would later promote as President. His proposals extended workmen's compensation and increased public works and highway spending. In 1931, he called a special session of the legislature to ask for $20,000,000 in unemployment relief; an increase in personal income taxes and the creation of a state relief agency. [3]

As the Depression deepened, the nation looked around for someone that had responded to the problems facing the people. Roosevelt had done that.

During the 1932 Presidential election campaign, Roosevelt was vague on the specifics of his "comprehensive program" designed to cure the ills of America. He did talk about areas that he wanted to get the national government involved in -- unemployment relief, legislation to shore up the railroads and agriculture, and plans to protect consumers and investors.

The most remarkable item of his campaign proposals was his pledge to cut government expenditures and balance the national budget. Roosevelt found it impossible to accomplish these two sets of promises.

His promises to take effective action carried the day, however. The dawn of big government had arrived.

Roosevelt's Inauguration and the beginnings of change

In March of 1933, Roosevelt was inaugurated and began the longest service as President in the history of our nation. In his first inaugural address, the President outlined what he thought was the most urgent problem facing the country and his philosophy for remedying the situation.

In his address, he stated, "Our greatest primary task is to put people to work...It can be accomplished in part by direct recruiting by the government itself, treating the task as we would treat the emergency of war,..." [4]

Here, in one sentence is President Roosevelt's primary answer to the problems facing our nation -- national government intervention. At that early stage, however, he was careful to include the states in his plans when he said, "I shall presently urge upon a new Congress in special session detailed measures...and I shall seek the immediate assistance of the Several States." [5]

President Roosevelt's statements provide insight into the situation as he saw it. He viewed the Great Depression as the primary enemy of our country. His references conjure up the image of joining together to fight common enemies -- poverty and despair. In this light, it possible to understand his thoughts on the extension of national power.

Previously, in times of crises dating as far back as the War for Independence, we had given up some areas of power and allowed it to be centralized to achieve a common goal. Roosevelt equated the depression with war and used it to justify these additional grants of national power.

Unfortunately, this marked a dramatic step away from the evolution of our form of government. The first powers secured by the national government were necessary to enable the national government to survive and to enable it to carry out its specified duties.

With President Roosevelt came the assertion that the national government must take additional powers in order to satisfy the objectives of a specific group of people. Granted, the depression effected all Americans. Granted, too, is the fact that Roosevelt had been elected by an overwhelming majority of Americans.

Yet problems of national scope do not necessarily confer additional powers upon the federal government. Additional powers are to be the result of specific grants of power from the people speaking through their states in the form of a constitutional amendment. No amendments were ever approved in support of the programs of President Roosevelt. The additional power came as the result of congressional action, executive decree and, later, judicial interpretation.

Roosevelt's actions not only resulted in an immediate

expansion of the powers of the national government, they also set a precedent that future Congresses and Presidents rely on.

The Hundred Days and Their Implication for the Future

During the period that came to be known as the Hundred Days, the new Congress acted quickly to carry out the new President's agenda. On March 9, both houses of Congress convened in special session. Their first order of business was the President's emergency banking bill. The purpose of this act and its provisions was to restore faith in the banks by guaranteeing deposits and preventing weak banks from reopening.

On March 16, the President asked for the Agricultural Adjustment Act. This act was one of the most far-reaching bills ever requested from Congress during peacetime. It provided for crop curtailment to reduce surpluses and refinancing of farm mortgages.

On March 21, the President asked for the creation of a Civilian Conservation Corps (CCC). The CCC had as its mission areas such as building dams, highways and reforestation projects. The unemployed would be given jobs in these areas and paid by the federal government. Here was an example of the President's "direct recruiting." That same day, the President asked for federal grants that would relieve unemployment. These funds were slated to go to the states.

On March 29, he asked Congress to pass legislation that would enable the national government to provide federal supervision of new securities that would be sold in interstate commerce.

Additionally, on April 10, President Roosevelt asked Congress to create the Tennessee Valley Authority. The TVA was to develop the power resources of the Tennessee River. This involved major federal investment.

On May 4, the President asked for powers to appoint a coordinator of transportation to encourage reorganization of the financial structures of railroad companies.

On May 12, he asked for the creation of a Federal Emergency Relief Agency. As part of its funding, it enabled the

Reconstruction Finance Corporation to supply the states with up to 500 million dollars. The FERA and its leader, Harry Hopkins, are the subject of an in-depth look later in this chapter.

On May 17, the President asked Congress for a broad range of tools that he thought were needed to stimulate the economy. Some of his proposals were to shorten the work week, establish a minimum wage, and prevent overproduction and unfair competition by means of fair-practice codes for each industry.

This plan also called for additional powers that would enable him to establish an employment program with an estimated 3.3 billion dollars to go into construction of public works programs.

While this legislation was not passed as presented, it was eventually approved on June 16th as the National Industrial Recovery Act.

There were other measures proposed during the 100 days. These reported actions were representative. Viewed collectively, they send a mixed message on exactly what the President was trying to accomplish. A few presented budget cuts -- the vast number authorize tremendous additional federal expenditures. Roosevelt promised to balance the federal budget in his 1932 campaign -- how he thought he could accomplish this and still implement the vast array of social programs remains a mystery.

It is unlikely that many members of that new Congress asked the basic question: Do we have the constitutional authority to expand the powers of the national government into these areas? There were some charges of socialism and many contended that the budget would not support the programs. These charges, however, are inflammatory on the one hand and mechanical on the other. No where did they ever decide to look at the real issue of ultimate power.

Roosevelt addressed his request for additional powers to the Congress -- a good many of whom owed their election to his popularity. It was as if Roosevelt was asking Congress to delegate some of its latent powers to deal with the crises. In reality, it was not Congress's approval that was necessary -- but the people's. President Roosevelt's request for expansion of federal authority should have been in the form of a proposed constitutional amendment. This did not occur and the distasteful result is that the country never had the opportunity to debate these issues. The additional grants of power were made "in Washington" effectively by-passing the state governments and the sovereignty that they represent.

President Roosevelt demonstrated how far he had moved by the time of his second inaugural. By that time, the worst of the crisis had passed. A great many Americans were back at work and industry was showing signs of recovery. Into this situation, President Roosevelt then projected an even broader call for American national government.

In his second inaugural message, he stated that, "Instinctively we recognized a deeper need - the need to find through government the instant of our united purpose to solve for the individual the ever-rising problems of a complex civilization." [6]

This is a radical departure from the concepts upon which our government was founded. For the first time, a President asserted that it is the responsibility of national government to intervene to solve the vast majority of problems facing its citizens. He goes even further; the implication is that the "ever-rising problems" will create the need for an ever-expanding sphere of influence for our national government.

If there is any doubt about FDR's intentions for the future of national government, one need look only further into the second inaugural address when he states that, "I see a United States which can demonstrate that, under democratic methods of government, national wealth can be translated into a spreading volume of human comforts hitherto unknown, and the lowest standard of living can be raised far above the level of mere subsistence." [7]

President Roosevelt's intentions are clear in this statement. He envisions a nation that spends its resources to increase the standard of living for everyone. This is noble-sounding but the effort encounters difficulty from the beginning. Obviously this national wealth must be collected before it can be "spread." To whom did the President look to collect this wealth -- the people. There has never been any real question about the necessity of assisting those that are unable to provide for themselves. The difficult questions center around who is in the best position to provide this aid.

There are other problems inherent in President Roosevelt's philosophy. In the process of gathering and distributing this "national wealth," many people will be hired and dollars will be spent. These people will be reluctant to give up their positions and will seek to protect them. The result will be an ever-expanding government bureaucracy. This is exactly what is happening today. Its genesis was with the administration of FDR and has continued to this day.

Yet another impact of the Roosevelt Administration and the Hundred Days has been the gradual intrusion into other areas of government. As mentioned, trends in government, once begun, are difficult to reverse. The national government has gone further and further into these fields. The results have not necessarily been clear laws. Often, the resulting laws are more complex -- these require further clarification -- opening up other areas to federal government expansion.

The Roosevelt Administration and the States

Federalism is the doctrine of dual sovereignty under which one group of people are served by two levels of government: national and state; each with its specific areas of power. The policies of the Roosevelt Administration went far to erase the lines that separated these two levels of government. Further, this time period saw the encroachment of the federal government into areas never conceived of by those that created the system. Under the guise of providing assistance to the people, federal administrators were given incredible coercive powers over the state governments. Here again, precedents for the relationship between the national and state governments were established. These precedents are difficult to reverse.

The Federal Emergency Relief Administration was created as part of Roosevelt's 100 days. It stemmed from his belief that only federal help could relieve the suffering of the unemployed in America. As it was set up originally, $250,000,000 was to comprise the federal match in assisting state relief efforts. Under the formula, the states would contribute $3 for every dollar of federal money. The act also set up an additional $250,000,000 discretionary fund that could be used in the form of block grants to assist people in states in advanced stages of need.

In order for the states to receive either matching or grant funds, they were required to provide "adequate administration." These centralized state relief agencies quickly became a permanent part of state government.

There are numerous examples of other kinds of pressure that was brought to bear on state governments during the early years of the FERA. In one instance, the federal agents in West Virginia decided that the state had exaggerated its inability to contribute its part in relief efforts. Since West Virginia had a good credit rating and a low tax structure, they decided that the problem was one of political cowardice. The FERA Administrator, Harry Hopkins, ordered Governor Herman Kump to call the state legislature into session to raise taxes or face the takeover of the state's relief efforts.

Hopkins was no kinder to other states. In 1934, after a dispute with Governor Bill Murray of Oklahoma, Hopkins federalized the relief efforts in the state. He followed this up by federalizing the relief program in Ohio a short-time later.

Imagine the situation -- officers of the federal government threatening governors to gain compliance of their interpretation of national laws. Then, if the conflict is not settled to their satisfaction, they "federalize" the relief effort.

The decision to federalize was not by the Supreme Court based on constitutional law. Nor even was it made by Congress acting under its legitimate interest in interstate commerce. The decision was made by a bureaucrat -- who used his own judgement as to the interpretation of a national law. The precedent established by this kind of activity is ominous. It raises several interesting questions -- what would happen to state government if the federal government decided that any state benefit was not funded at the proper level? Could they federalize that program? Mr. Hopkins might have answered "yes."

The administration of FDR impacted other areas, too. The

WPA (Works Project Administration) was a major federal program that acted directly on the people. Although the WPA was helpful, it began the pattern of direct reliance on the federal government. Like the FERA, it was also a product of the 100 days. It gave relief to those able to work while leaving to the states the responsibility for the relief of unemployables.

Many of the new programs were passed between 1933 and immediately after FDR's reelection in 1936. The SEC and the CCC (Civilian Conservation Corps) were federal programs that had no state participation. The National Labor Relations Board, the Agricultural Adjustment Administration and the Farm Security Administration also by- passed state action.

The REA (Rural Electricfication Agency) and the FHA required only minimum state action. An even more overt attempt to subvert the will of the states was taken in the case of the United States Housing Administration. On this issue, liberal Congressmen deliberately enacted programs that entailed federal-local and not federal-state relationships -- thereby by-passing rurally-controlled state legislatures.

The relationship between the national and state governments was a very difficult one during these times. The federal bureaucrats, armed with the popularity of Roosevelt, went forth from Washington prepared to impose their will on the states. It was true that many state governments were dominated by rural interests. These leaders had no intention of raising taxes on their impoverished constituents to support the problems of the cities. The bureaucrats often complained about having to deal with anti-New Deal lobbyists in the state capitals that "hated progressive taxation, labor unions and costly welfare laws."

Often, these federal agents sought to use coercion to accomplish their goals (as in the case of FERA and Hopkins). Other ideas submitted by the field agents was their ability to control the states through the 150,000 jobs available through patronage. This proposal was another hot topic as it would have placed these jobs at the disposal of federal bureaucrats and not the locally elected officials of the states.

Occasionally, these efforts to control the states ran into stubborn opposition. Some "ultra-conservative" governors lashed out at the interference by the federal government and threatened to refuse the "tainted money" from Washington.

In other instances, the states actually won the confrontation. One notable occasion occurred in both 1933 and 1935 when Governor Eugene Talmadge of Georgia refused to cooperate with the Federal Bureau of Roads and dared President Roosevelt to cut off highway funds. FDR backed down.

These victories, however, were few and far between. For the most part, the administration of FDR pressed on -- unhampered -- in its efforts to change the American political landscape. The real issue to consider is the impact that these programs had on federalism, itself. They affected federalism in many ways: These programs established a dominance by the national government in the areas that most directly affect the people -- areas such as unemployment, welfare, and social security.

These programs could have easily been enacted and effectively operated by state governments -- some of them had been. Before the election of Roosevelt, eight states had already established relief efforts.

By 1935, all but 13 states had some sort of assistance for the elderly. Slowly but surely, the states were already responding to the social needs of the country. The entrance of the national government into these areas restricted the future action of the states. This in itself has had a long-lasting impact on the states.

The entry of the federal government into these areas also meant that the federal government would have to increase its income. It did this through higher income taxes. The use of this source of income by the national government effectively prevented the states from entry into this area -- thereby denying the states a good portion of the income that they needed to support these programs.

All-tolled, the spending on welfare increased 300% during the decade of the 1930s. This spending brought with it a corresponding increase in the debt of government.

During the same time period, the national debt increased from 16.4 to 43.4 billion dollars; state debt increased from 2.4 to 3.5 billion dollars and local debt increased from 15.6 to 16.7 billion dollars. This huge debt increase, particularly at the national level, is a problem that we continue to face today. Social programs were a major cause of this debt and once added, these programs are among the most difficult to reduce or eliminate from the budget -- even if the need arises to do so.

During the New Deal, the national government sought to right wrongs that were not the responsibility of any individual or group of individuals. These problems were attributed to "society." The federal government accepted blame for many of the troubles that confronted the nation. Since the problem faced society, the federal government surmised that there was a need for federal intervention.

The role of the national government as an intervenor for all of society's problems was never envisioned by the framers of our Constitution. The burden is just too great. For our government to attempt to right these wrongs is just not possible or necessary. This would require an unlimited amount of authority (and money) to combat an unlimited array of problems. Unfortunately, this is an another of the problems that stems directly from the FDR administration. He believed that by the use of national wealth the standard of living could be raised for everyone. To achieve this, he initiated the tax and spend philosophy that we have today.

It did more than just involve the federal government in a series of unconstitutional acts, it raised the expectations of the people towards their federal government and its role in solving problems.

While the expansion of federal authority was originally espoused by President Roosevelt, it was eventually upheld by the United States Supreme Court. Their decisions played a vital role in the transformation.

The New Deal and the Supreme Court

At the beginning of the New Deal, the United States Supreme Court was made up of elderly, conservative justices. Their age would seem to be unimportant, but as the New Deal progressed it became a major factor in the ability of the Court to maintain its independence and its role as guardian of the Constitution.

It is understandable that the first actions of Congress in their Hundred Days and the torrent of "social legislation" would come under fire. The country had never been exposed to this kind of activist national government -- except during war-time. When the people were confronted with sweeping changes that flew in the face of the traditional role of our government, challenges arose.

Originally, the Supreme Court held that a good many of these new programs were unconstitutional. One of those programs struck down by the Court in May of 1935 was the National Industrial Recovery Act (NRA). This act was signed into law by President Roosevelt on June 16, 1933. Included in this act was the largest grant of peacetime powers to control industrial wages, hours and prices.

Roosevelt termed this as "an emergency job", designed to meet the needs of putting people back to work. One of the measures that the President felt was needed to revitalize the nation included the authority to license individual industries if they disregarded a set of voluntary fair competition codes. The impact of this provision would be to nationalize these industries.

Since most of these powers were conferred on the President and his designates in the Executive Branch of the national government, this grant of power was almost dictatorial in nature.

Immediately, challenges arose to various aspects of this law. The case that actually resulted in the invalidation of this law was brought by the A.L.A. Schecter Live Poultry Company of Brooklyn (Schecter Corp. v. United States). They questioned the right of the national government to fix wages and hours of labor.

To this, the Court responded, that, "Extraordinary conditions may call for extraordinary remedies. But extraordinary conditions do not create or enlarge constitutional power." The discretion of the President in approving or prescribing laws for the government of trade and industry throughout the country is virtually unfettered. We think that the code-making authority thus conferred is an unconstitutional delegation of legislative power."

83

"In determining how far the Federal Government may go in controlling intrastate transactions upon the ground that they "affect" interstate commerce, there is a necessary and well-established distinction between direct and indirect effects. Otherwise there would be virtually no limit to the Federal Power and for all practical purposes we would have a completely centralized government." ... "We are of the opinion that the attempt through the provisions of the code to fix the hours and wages of employees of defendants in their intrastate business was not valid exercise of Federal Power."

An even more far-reaching statement in the decision was that, "It is not the providence of the court to consider the economic advantage of such a centralized government. It is sufficient to say that the federal Constitution does not provide for it."

This was one of the last major decisions limiting the power of the national government during the Roosevelt administration. In it, the Court had upheld the concept of federalism and specifically the Tenth Amendment. Like the framers of the Constitution, this Court recognized the dangers of an all powerful centralized government.

Immediately after Roosevelt's reelection in 1936, he decided that he needed to have a Supreme Court that was friendly to his New Deal proposals. To accomplish this, he sent a message to Congress of February 5 of 1937. This message was entitled "Reorganization of the Judicial Branch of the Government."

This proposal has come to be known as his "court-packing scheme" because in it, he proposed that Congress give him the power to appoint one additional justice for every justice then over seventy years of age (at the time of his proposal, six of the Justices were seventy or over).

President Roosevelt had couched his proposal in language that indicated that he merely wanted to give these aging justices assistance but his real purpose was clear. He wanted to recreate the Supreme Court to support his New Deal legislation. His proposal was overwhelmingly defeated on July 22. While this was his first major legislative defeat, the damage to the Supreme Court had already been done.

The Supreme Court of the United States began to reverse its stand on FDR's proposals -- not as the result of any new findings of law, but because they had been threatened by the President.

On April 12, 1937, the Court decided in favor of allowing the government to retain sweeping powers over employer-employee relations with its decision in the case of the National Labor Relations Board v. Jones & Laughlin Steel Corp.

In this case, the Jones & Laughlin Steel Corporation had refused to reinstate and pay back wages to ten employees that it had discharged. The NLRB argued that these employees had been fired because of their union involvement.

The argument used by the government was that the NLRB had been created to diffuse tension in the labor force by sanctioning discussions between unions and employers. The NLRB was predicated on the principal that industrial strife could lead to problems in interstate commerce.

The arguments put forward by the FDR administration were obviously strained. The slimness of these arguments was pointed out by the attorneys for the steel company when they stated that, "There has been no strike or labor dispute in the present case. In actuality, the petitioner (government) means that the (discharge of these ten employees) might have led to dissatisfaction, which might have led to a labor dispute, which might have led to a strike (which might have resulted in) a consequent interruption of interstate commerce."

The steel corporation, on the other hand, relied on the historical evolution of our government from its inception; including a direct reliance on the findings in the Schecter case that dismantled the NRA.

The Justices, however, caved in to the pressure. Reading the opinion, you can still hear the defensiveness of the justices. At one point, regarding the interpretation of the statute, the opinion states, "We have repeatedly held that as between two possible interpretations of a statute, by one of which it would be unconstitutional and the other valid, our plain duty is to adopt that which will save the act."

Here, they concede that the act is unconstitutional but state that they will use an interpretation that they can uphold. The phrase, "We have repeatedly held..." indicates the defensive posture of this decision, so close to the court-packing proposal of the President. In their opinion, the Court ignores its own conclusions about the difference between "direct and indirect effects" on interstate commerce. Rather than decide on the merits of the law, which could be applied to almost any industry; they decided the constitutionality on the basis of the size of the business involved in the suit. The steel corporation had operations in several states. The Court upheld the validity of the act not for its own merit but because the business involved in this specific case had interstate dealings.

Once the floodgates were opened by this decision, others quickly followed. Probably one of the most important of these was the case of Helvering v. Davis; which was decided later that year on May 24, 1937.

This case involved the Social Security Act of 1935. From this decision came legal support for almost any future incursion of federal powers.

In this case, the Supreme Court predicated its decision on several factors. The first of these was that, "security for the aged, like the general problems of unemployment, is national as well as local."

After having defined the problem as national and local (state), the Court went on the make a determination that the state might not move to solve it. Their reasoning was that, "State governments ae reluctant to place such heavy burdens upon their residents lest they incur economic disadvantages..."

These two arguments are irrelevant to the basic question of the right of the federal government to act in this area. The Court noted that the problem was both national and local. They did not even assert that the problem was solely national. Even if it were, "extraordinary conditions do not create or enlarge constitutional power."

After giving the national government a share of the responsibility, the Court then decides that the states may not act. (In fact, at that time, all but 13 already had some sort of provisions for support of the elderly.) This supposition is clearly outside the role of the Supreme Court as guardian of the Constitution.

An admission that a problem exists -- and that the problem is national does not carry with it the absolute right of the national government to act if the states have not. As has been stated previously, a problem may be national -- but it is subject to national control only by the approval of the people in the form of a constitutional amendment.

The third point, however, may be the most important. The government had argued that Congress had the power to enact this measure under Article I, Section 8, cl. 1 which enables it to "lay and collect taxes, duties, impost and excises, to pay the debts and provide for the common defense and general welfare of the United States." Historically, this phrase had never been construed to mean that Congress could provide for individuals compromising the United States but only for the general welfare of their union.

The hard-pressed Court decided in this case that the concept of "general welfare" is not static but adapts itself to the crises and necessities of time. Their specific words were that, "Nor is the concept of the general welfare static. Needs that were narrow or parochial a century ago may be interwoven in our day with the well-being of the nation. What is critical or urgent changes with the times."

Here, they reversed themselves and they changed the trend of history. From this decision, the federal government has been given the power to determine what constitutes the general welfare of the nation. This power would be used to involve the national government in an ever- broadening circle of activities. In this decision, the Justices rewrote the Constitution. This instance, as had been the case in previous occurrences, was for a good purpose -- providing for the elderly in America. But the method was wrong. Once this interpretation was introduced, it would not go away.

On paper, FDR's court-packing scheme appeared to fail. In reality, it may have been his most lasting success.

By the late 1930s, the nation's attention was diverted from economic matters by the events in Europe and Asia. The ominous clouds of war were on the horizon and war preparations began in earnest. Of course, no one protested the strengthening of the national government as it sought to protect America from foreign enemies -- this was both necessary and proper.

The coming of the Second World War eliminated most of the economic problems that faced our nation. It also ended the debate over the role of the federal government. Over the next twenty years, the major concern of government would be foreign policy and the Cold War with the Communist-bloc nations. The newly created domestic programs would become quietly entrenched and part of our political landscape.

But the tone had been set. When the next activist President was elected in 1960, he would find that most of the groundwork had been laid. President John F. Kennedy and his successor, Lyndon Baines Johnson would construct an even larger, more pervasive federal colossus on this foundation.

CHAPTER EIGHT

THE KENNEDY-JOHNSON ERA

The last years of President Franklin Roosevelt were spent guiding America through the Second World War. President Harry S. Truman shared these responsibilities and inherited the drastically different world that resulted from that war.

While President Truman intended to move the country in the direction of greater national government involvement, the Congress refused, for the most part, to pass his Fair Deal legislation.

Most of his time was spent dealing with the international situation and American efforts to rebuild Europe.

In 1952, the country turned to its military hero, General Dwight D. Eisenhower, for leadership. President Eisenhower inherited the Korean War from President Truman. He, too, was primarily involved in the foreign affairs of the nation.

The Eisenhower era was a time of tranquility. After the Korean War, the nation was at peace -- and very prosperous. The President was not vigorous in his leadership and the vast majority of the people were content with a quiescent national government -- for a change.

President Eisenhower led no assault on the New Deal programs -- and, in fact, the Department of Health, Education and Welfare was established early in his administration. For the most part the President pursued a calm, non-expansionist policy.

The President as a Voice For Change

By a slim margin, John F. Kennedy defeated Eisenhower's Vice President, Richard M. Nixon, and was elected President in 1960. He accomplished this feat, in part, by challenging Americans to shake off their lethargy.

He represented Alexander Hamilton's theory of "energetic government." President Kennedy presented some ideas as to what he thought America might accomplish with its national wealth and power -- he communicated these thoughts to the American people and encouraged them to see his vision.

Above all, he was a communicator. His support of an issue gave it instant credibility. But it was not the accomplishments of his administration that had the great impact on our system of government. In fact he, like his predecessors, was most interested in the international situation. All but three paragraphs of his inaugural address dealt with international issues.

Events such as the Bay of Pigs, Berlin and the Cuban Missile Crisis quickly forced President Kennedy to put foreign affairs at the top of his priority list. He did believe in the expansion of the role of the federal government. There is ample evidence to support this -- and it will be discussed later. (He was not very successful in attaining legislative success, however.)

It would be up to his successor, Lyndon Baines Johnson, to make many of President Kennedy's dreams into reality. In truth, the greatest devotee to the philosophy of President Kennedy may well have been his Vice President. Between the two of them, they radically altered the balance of power between the states and the national government.

"Now the trumpet summons us again -- not as a call to bear arms, though arms we need -- not as a call to battle, though embattled we are -- but a call to bear the burden of a long twilight struggle, year in and year out, "rejoicing in hope, patient in tribulation" -- a struggle against the common enemies of man: tyranny, poverty, disease and war itself." From Kennedy's Inaugural.

By these words, President Kennedy sought to include the issues of poverty and disease among the other great enemies of personal liberty. Earlier, remember, the precedent had been established by President Franklin Roosevelt when he equated the Great Depression with war. The question was, how did President Kennedy intend to attack these kinds of problems? The answer lies with John Maynard Keynes, a noted British economist.

Kennedy and Keynes

John Maynard Keynes (1883-1946) is credited with originating the monetary policy upon which most of the free world is operated. In his General Theory of Employment, Interest and Money (published in 1936), Keynes argued that government had a responsibility to actively combat economic problems. His solution to recessions and depressions was for government to spend more money and to make money more available through easy credit (lower interest rates and more money available for loans).

His underlying theory was that high levels of consumer demand were necessary to achieve full employment and economic growth. The essence of this school of thought is that the government must engage in deficit spending practices to ensure a healthy economy. The debate between those that favor Keynes' "demand side" theories and those that favor "supply side" are too detailed to be discussed here. Yet, it is important to understand that President Kennedy advocated "demand side" economics for the government.

President Kennedy has been described as the "first Keynesian President" by one of his strongest supporters." [1]

This same account went on to add that Kennedy learned his economics during the later days of the New Deal when this Keynesian revolution was having its first effect. "This saved him from being taught that government intervention in the economy was wicked or that a balanced budget should be the supreme goal of economic policy." [2]

One of the Kennedy's objectives as President was to achieve full employment without inflation. He decided that the way to do this was to adhere to his Keynesian background and run the national government with unbalanced budgets. In this, he sought and quickly found support in the European economies of the day.

By one account, Kennedy "...soon discovered that western Europe was happily free of the American budgetary obsession." [3]

And that the Treasurer-General of the Netherlands, E. Van Lenep, said that, "In Europe one does not understand why in the

United States there is still a strong tendency to have a balanced budget as a target.." [4]

The President's commitment to the philosophy of government spending is clearly demonstrated in his 1962 Economic Report where he states that "Growth will require increased public investment, just as it will require increased private investment...We must face the question of public versus private expenditures pragmatically, in terms of intrinsic merits and costs, not in terms of fixed preconceptions." [5]

One of the "fixed preconceptions" that the President referred to is the principle that most of us live by -- if you spend more than you earn, someday you will run out of money. This was exactly what happened to the national government -- in a very short time.

By this time, Kennedy was convinced that to achieve his goal of full employment and no inflation that government spending (and deficit spending) was the answer. There are two ways to achieve a deficit -- one is to cut taxes and the other is to increase spending. There were efforts to do both in the Kennedy Administration.

Kennedy and Social Legislation

One approach advocated by President Kennedy was to increase government expenditures by increasing the national government's responsibilities and workforce.

In the spring of 1961, he began a series of messages with the intention of educating the public as to some of the needs for social legislation. His first message was on Health and Hospital Care (on February 9); followed by messages on Education (February 20); Natural Resources (February 23); Highways (February 28); Housing and Community Development (March 9); and an Omnibus Message on Urgent National Needs on May 25. In later years, messages were added on a variety of other issues: civil rights, transportation, public welfare, consumer protection, mental illness, youth and the elderly. [6]

The vast majority of these issues were not acted upon during his presidency -- but they were addressed. They became major issues -- and received attention through the efforts of President Kennedy. Moreover, his actions tended to put these issues in the national arena -- thereby implying the federal government's duty to address these areas of concern. With the exception of civil rights, none of these areas are to be found, even generally within the Constitution or subsequent amendments. Yet, by his efforts, President Kennedy sought to federalize these problems -- thereby further preempting action by private organizations and state government.

The President did gain approval on some of his "New Society" programs. On December 2, 1961, the President presented a special message to Congress that dealt with "social issues." Within six months of that time, Congress passed an area redevelopment bill, an omnibus housing bill, a farm bill, an increase in the minimum wage, the liberalization of social security benefits, temporary unemployment benefits, benefits to dependent children of unemployed parents and a program to combat water pollution -- this was a record unequaled on the domestic front since the New Deal days of 1935. [7]

In reality, some of these issues were probably "unfinished business" from the New Deal. As has been the case with many other expansive federal laws, some of them were both good and needed. The States, however, are in a better position to enact and administer these types of legislation and craft these laws to fit their individual needs.

This situation illustrates another problem, too -- these laws were not before Congress by virtue of a constitutional mandate -- but through the communication skills of a President. This is the difficulty with allowing the intent of the Constitution to be altered with the change of political administration.

Kennedy and the States

The final area where President Kennedy had a direct impact on the nature of federalism was in the views that he expressed towards the role of the national government in solving patently local problems.

On the domestic side, Kennedy had an understanding of

urban and industrial issues -- these were the areas where he was most at home. [8]

It is natural for people to tend to the familiar -- for that reason, it might be expected that a great many of the domestic issues addressed by the President would have been in these areas. Indeed this was the case.

Early in his term, he began encouraging the creation of a new Cabinet Department -- a Department of Housing and Urban Affairs. The federal government already had the responsibility for one city, Washington, D.C. This department was to have the responsibility for advocating the interests of the cities all over the country. The President's Special Message to Congress wherein he suggested the establishment of this department is a concise synopsis of his thinking and the kinds of intrusive programs that he envisioned for the country.

Barely had his message begun when he began to state his philosophy of the relative roles of the different levels of government, "I propose to act now to strengthen and improve the machinery through which, in large part, the Federal Government must act to carry out its proper role of encouragement and assistance to States and local governments, to voluntary efforts and to private enterprise, in the solution of these problems."

This role of "encouragement and assistance" resulted in a federal takeover of a local activity -- namely caring for the special needs of a community. Later in the document, the President stated that he felt that the problems of the cities were national problems. "We will neglect our cities at our peril, for in neglecting them we neglect the nation."

There were those who questioned the fairness of increased taxing of rural people to pay for improving the lives of those that live in the cities.

This did more than add additional expenses to the federal government; it also began to single out the larger cities for preferential treatment. Further, this concept would eliminate much of the dialogue between the Mayor and the State House. Now, the Mayor was to do business directly with Washington -- by passing the states and weakening their power.

This does not even begin to address the fact that no where in our Constitution is the national government empowered to act on behalf of the cities at the expense of the rest of the country (or even to act on behalf of the cities at all.) Remember that cities existed at the time of the drafting of our Constitution. Even then, they were understood to have different needs than the countryside. Thomas Jefferson, you will recall, was an advocate of a totally agrarian society while Alexander Hamilton was a man of the cities.

The final difficulty forced on the nation by this approach was found in the conclusion of this message. President Kennedy had ironically submitted this plan under the Reorganization Act of 1949 which attempted to encourage efficiency in government. Reorganizations were to result in cost-savings to the taxpayers. Note the language in the close of the President's address, "Although the taking effect of the reorganization provided for in the reorganization plan will not in itself result in immediate savings, the improvement achieved in administration will in the future allow the performance of necessary services at greater savings than present operations would permit. An itemization of these savings in advance of the actual experience is not practicable."

Here in the space of one message, the President has summed up how far our national government had moved from the intentions of those that created it.

As the President had stated in his message, uncharted areas were to be open to the federal government because it had to "carry out its proper role in encouragement and assistance to States and local governments..." In short, the national government could act because it wanted to.

Finally, this administration clearly indicated that it did not intend to maintain fiscally sound principles in money management. The decision was to spend -- without regard for the impact on the financial soundness of the nation and the American taxpayer. All of this notwithstanding, it is not accurate to hold President Kennedy totally responsible for the huge mushrooming federal establishment. Even his much sought after Department of Housing and Urban Affairs was not passed during his Presidency. In fact, his effectiveness rating with

Congress was not very high (only a 27% success ratio in 1963, for example).

Ironically, it was not during Kennedy's time in the Oval Office that had the greatest impact on the issue of federalism -- although it was his vision. The real activity came after his untimely death and the ascendency of Lyndon Johnson to the Presidency. While many liberals condemned Lyndon Johnson as being against their beliefs, his Presidency soon proved their fears to be wrong.

Johnson had been listening to President Kennedy; he accepted many of Kennedy's ideas -- and further, he had the legislative skill necessary to make those programs into a reality. The tragedy of Kennedy's death evoked in the country and Congress the feeling that there was "unfinished business" from the Kennedy years. Johnson used this theme to press for these programs.

Lyndon B. Johnson accepted the Kennedy approach to government and expanded the national government to new areas. Under President Johnson and his program called the "Great Society," the federal government continued to usurp powers from the states.

The Background of Lyndon Johnson

Discussions of the Presidency of Lyndon Johnson almost invariably turn into a recitation of his failings in foreign policy -- specifically the conduct of the Vietnam war. While much of his attention was focused on this conflict, he was also focusing on expanding the federal bureaucracy with the corresponding expansion of both taxes and the budget deficit.

With changes in domestic policy came a continual lessening of the freedom of the states. This was a result of the main thrust of the Johnson years -- more national government to cure all of our ills and federal tax dollars to address the issues of the day.

Lyndon Baines Johnson was a curious mix of independent Texan and avid New Dealer. Born on August 27, 1908 in a farmhouse in central Texas, Johnson had somewhat of a frontier upbringing.

His early years were far from easy -- he worked as a janitor and borrowed money to go to college. After his graduation in 1930, he immediately turned his attention to politics. He went to Washington as the secretary to a Texas Congressman, Richard M. Kleburg and held this position for four years.

In 1935, President Roosevelt appointed Johnson as the National Youth Administration state administrator for Texas. Here, he had the opportunity to observe the inside of the New Deal.

In 1937, Johnson resigned his post with the NYA to seek a term as a Congressman in a special election. Johnson took a strong advocacy position of FDR's policies; including his court-packing scheme. His opponents were opposed to a continuation of most of the New Deal policies. Johnson triumphed over nine better-known opponents and was elected. Immediately after that election, FDR and Johnson met and established a lasting friendship.

In 1941, Johnson made his first effort for a United States Senate seat and lost by a mere 1,311 votes. In his second effort in 1948, Johnson won by an even slimmer 87 votes and took his place in the Senate. Once in the Senate, Johnson made his mark immediately. In 1953, Johnson was elected as the Minority Leader and when his party regained control of the Senate in 1954, he was elected as Majority Leader.

In the Senate, he was characterized as a genius in the legislative process by Senator (and later Vice President) Hubert H. Humphrey. In the ability to get legislation approved, Johnson had few peers. This insight proved valuable to him when he became President.

His election as Kennedy's Vice President in 1960 brought him back into the executive branch of government where he would remain for the rest of his public life. It was here that he was exposed to the ideas and goals of President Kennedy.

In the Senate, Johnson had been a moderate. As Vice President, he had little opportunity to shape policy. His sudden elevation to President gave him the opportunity to work once again with the Congress and propose legislation which would change the landscape of American government.

President Lyndon B. Johnson took some of Kennedy's ideas on the need for expansion of the federal government, added quite a few of his own -- and produced the greatest torrent of social legislation since the New Deal. His program was called the Great Society. Toward the end of his presidency, even Johnson knew that it had failed.

Johnson and the Great Society

To understand the intention of President Johnson and his Great Society, it is essential to know his view of the role of the federal government. One commentator on the Johnson Presidency wrote that, "In political philosophy, President Johnson seems to have pictured this vista: The federal government will legislate comprehensively -- really, without limit -- for the people's own good, whether they have yet come to recognize the need or not." [9]

Here is the fruition of the dream of Alexander Hamilton's energetic government and the nightmare of Thomas Jefferson and all of the others who had long labored to prevent this type of unchecked central authority.

A partial listing of Johnson's legislative triumphs during the 1966 and 1967 legislative sessions is enough to give a clear picture of the kinds of new programs (and expansions of old programs) that appeared -- almost from nowhere -- and became national laws.

In 1966, the programs included: Food for India, child nutrition, the creation of the Department of Transportation, truth in packaging laws, model cities, rent supplements, Teachers Corps, clean rivers, child safety, narcotics rehabilitation, highway safety, traffic safety, mine safety, bail reform, tire safety, another increase in the minimum wage, urban mass transit, federal aid to highways and water research. [10]

For 1967, the list is almost as detailed: The Education Act, control of air pollution, Partnership for Health, increases in Social Security, age discrimination, wholesome meat, flammable fabrics, urban research, public broadcasting, Blind-

Deaf Center, college work-study, summer youth program and food stamps. [11]

As with many of the laws mentioned previously -- many of these are good laws -- deserving support. Many others are grounded in good intentions -- but their enactment has increased the burden of the federal government. This preempted state legislatures from acting on these issues and also wreaked havoc on the federal budget.

Another complicating factor was the President's continuing support of the efforts to thwart communism in southeast Asia. In his 1965 Inaugural Address, President Johnson prepared the nation for the escalating conflict with these words -- "If American lives must end, and American treasure be spilled, in countries that we barely know, then that is the price that change has demanded of conviction and of our enduring covenant."

Our involvement in Viet Nam, coupled with the expense of Johnson's programs, proved very costly to our future financial stability.

It has been said that a nation cannot have both guns (military strength) and butter (social programs) at the same time. Yet, this is precisely what President Johnson proposed to do. As late in his term as 1966, he proclaimed that the nation could and would spend for both military and domestic needs. "Both of these commitments involve great costs. They are costs we can and will meet...The struggle in Vietnam must be supported. The advance toward a Great Society at home must be continued unabated." [12]

Part of this advance included another famous Johnson war -- the war on poverty. Again, notice that a domestic problem is labeled as a war to enable the federal government to step in with its vast resources. The aim of these programs was good -- even noble -- but they failed to have any significant impact on need in America. The pricetag for this failed effort has been substantial. During the Kennedy-Johnson Presidency, the total social-welfare expenditures at all levels went from 67 billion dollars to 127 billion dollars. And this was only the beginning.

The budgetary impact of the Johnson programs has refused to go away. One result of his approach to domestic issues was that the federal bureaucracy "blossomed" and it became more centralized. Federal employment in Washington increased by 41% during this time; federal jobs elsewhere by only 11%. Agencies with "regulatory" duties grew rapidly. A good example of these growth patterns can be found in the Department of Health, Education and Welfare. This department was created during Eisenhower's first term in 1953. Prior to the Kennedy-Johnson years, this department had a budget of 5.4 billion dollars and 35,000 employees.[13-14]

By 1980, this agency had grown to 150,000 employees and its programs accounted for two hundred billion dollars.[15]

Compounding the problems created by this growth was the attitude espoused by those that served in those agencies. They have been described as people who saw themselves as "'big brother' to a rather remote public."[16]

This bureaucracy left its indelible stamp on the future of public assistance by leaving future presidencies programs that "could no longer be restricted by state or local residency requirements, by whether there was an employable man in the house, or by realistic "needs" tests."[17]

The end result of these efforts was a huge, unwieldly federal bureaucracy largely unresponsive to both the general public and its officials in the executive branch of government.

The final charge that can be brought against this administration was the effect that it had on the financial health of the nation. In order to pay for all these varied activities, the Johnson Administration had increased the money supply -- this began to fuel inflation.

The consumer price index rose 18 points from 1963 through the end of this presidency; the interest rate to business doubled; and inflation became a permanent fixture of our economy because this administration failed to raise adequate revenue to support the programs.

These consequences were not unexpected, nor should they have been surprising. Remember that Thomas Jefferson had railed against a public debt as a mortgage on future generations. It seems inconceivable that the President, his chief economists, and many members of Congress could not foresee the consequences of these actions. In their shortsightedness, they left an inheritance that none of us would wish for -- a huge, almost uncontrollable national debt.

Unfortunately, too, this financial burden has hurt the most those that it sought to help. Inflation hits the poor the hardest -- their wages are lost quicker. Their dollar purchases less; government expenditures do not go quite as far. Indeed, this is likely a significant part of the Johnson legacy. Strive as he might to improve the conditions of the poor -- his policies may ultimately have done more harm than good.

The Johnson Epilogue

Toward the end of his presidency, surrounded by the protests of almost every interest group in the nation -- most of whom he had tried to help, President Johnson began to hear the bad news from those closest to him. The common thought was that Johnson's policies had gone too far, too fast. They simply had expanded far beyond their level of effectiveness and beyond the willingness of the people to pay.

As he was about to end his presidency, President Johnson and Senator Barry Goldwater (who Johnson had beaten in the 1964 Presidential race) had the opportunity to spend some time together. At that time, the President told Senator Goldwater that he knew that the Great Society programs were not working -- he was unsure of the reasons why. [18]

In structuring his Great Society programs, the President had hoped to raise the standard of living for America's citizens. Rather than provide incentives, his approach was for the federal government to right all of the ills of society. It was an impossible mission from the start.

In its concept -- it was an American dream. In a land of plenty, no one should want. But in its execution, it failed the President and those that it sought to serve. Worse than that, it left problems that are just beginning to be addressed. The Great Society was the culmination of widespread usurpation of authority by a centralized power.

The national government began to act without a true

mandate from the people. Its growth was spurred by unsound monetary policy and this legacy has imposed untold taxes on the future of all Americans. Individual freedoms were lessened and the counterbalancing power of the states was weakened. The bureaucracies at all levels of government grew and continue to grow, unchecked.

Every administration since that of Richard Nixon has been nominally pledged to reducing the negative aspects of the Great Society programs. This speaks volumes in defense of limited national government.

The Kennedy/Johnson Era, Education and Housing

Previously, we have discussed the Kennedy and Johnson administrations in general terms. To understand the impact that they had on the national government, some specific examples are necessary.

Two areas that demonstrate the result of their policies are education and housing. The federal government had been involved in both of these areas prior to these administrations -- but the scope of the involvement had been limited. With these Presidents, their role was greatly expanded -- and has continued to expand to this day.

While both of these areas are important to the nation, there is no explicit Constitutional authority for federal involvement. Here, as in other areas -- the first step into these new fields established a precedent.

Education

As defined by the federal government, there are two kinds of education; elementary and secondary education (including high schools) and higher education (colleges, universities and advanced technical training).

The first major involvement of the federal government was in the area of higher education. The passage of the first Morrill Act in 1862 was designed to aid in the formation of colleges to train students in agriculture and industrial education. (Even this proposal had a difficult time becoming law. Its first passage was by the slimmest of margins and it was vetoed by President James Buchanan as being unconstitutional. To encourage passage, Justin S. Morrill included provisions for military training. As the nation was involved in a civil war, President Abraham Lincoln signed the bill when it came before him.)

The first bureaucratic efforts at the national level occurred as the result of a memorial presented to Congress in 1866 by the National Association of State and City School Superintendents. They urged the creation of a federal education agency. This became a reality in March of 1867 when President Andrew Johnson approved legislation that created a "Department of Education." The mission of this office was to collect data on the status of education; to present information to aid the people in the establishment and maintenance of good schools and to promote education at all levels. [19]

This is a proper role for the national government. From its vantage point, it can provide needed information to those charged with the administration of education. Over time, it has expanded its role into direct involvement.

Along the way, a second Morrill Act was passed in 1890 -- this one to aid in the creation of black colleges.

The first concentrated involvement of the federal government in education occurred during the administration of President Franklin D. Roosevelt. The previously-mentioned FERA supported several different educational programs; as did the National Youth Administration (remember that Lyndon Johnson was active in this program). The Civilian Conservation Corps provided vocational education. The National Cancer Institute Act was the beginning of the policy of public health service fellowships.

For the most part, these programs were carried out as "aspects of relief." They gave jobs to out-of-work teachers and college students. The Public Works Administration also made grants and loans to states and local government for the purpose of buildings schools and college buildings. [20]

Despite all of these activities, education has been regarded as being in the domain of the states. In the enabling Acts of

Congress that provided for the admission of at least ten new states, exclusive authority over public education was reserved to them (under the principle of the Tenth Amendment). As late as the National Defense Act of 1958, the Congress reaffirmed this principle -- "declaring that the states and local communities have and must retain control over, and primary responsibility for, public education." [21]

Federal aid to education became a national political issue in 1960 in the election between John F. Kennedy and Richard M. Nixon. In the 1960 budget, the Eisenhower Administration had proposed a "modest" program of long-term loans for school construction. Opposition arose from liberal members of Congress who were looking to create a political issue. [22]

When the bill reached the Senate floor, it was amended to add a provision for increases in teacher's salaries. The vote was equally divided and Vice President Nixon cast the tie-breaking vote against the bill. This vote became an issue of the Presidential campaign of 1960 with John Kennedy attacking Nixon's vote in the first televised presidential debate. Nixon explained his vote in terms of the Tenth Amendment, "When the federal government gets the power to pay teachers, inevitably...it will require the power to set standards and to tell teachers what to teach." [23]

After his election, President Kennedy sought to expand the federal role in education and assumed active leadership in the efforts to achieve a general aid bill. The Administration submitted a permanent, multibillion dollar bill for salary and construction assistance. [24]

This proposal was defeated in the House Rules Committee -- largely over the question of federal support for parochial schools.

By 1963, the Administration had changed tactics. In that year, President Kennedy submitted an omnibus group of special aid proposals. This included "scholarships and construction aid for colleges, programs for libraries, adult education, vocational education at the elementary and secondary levels." [25]

The Congress then pieced together the most attractive parts of the program, skirting the controversial issues. This approach worked and the stage was set. These specific steps would result in the passage of a much broader education bill -- passed under the vigorous leadership of President Johnson.

This legislation, hailed as a "breakthrough," was passed in 1965 and was entitled the Elementary and Secondary Education Act (ESEA). This act, "began a new era in federal aid to education, doubling the federal share of elementary and secondary education expenditures and establishing a new pattern of intergovernmental relationships in education." [26]

Included in this legislation were programs to aid the educationally disadvantaged, provide classroom materials, promote innovation in education, support educational research, and assist state education agencies. [27]

The involvement of President Johnson in this success is duly noted in a comprehensive report on education, "Throughout the long history of struggle for federal aid, Congress had been the traditional focus of activity. Yet, ESEA was plainly the product of executive initiative, part of a broad Presidential agenda to combat poverty." [28]

This bill was indeed comprehensive and costly. For its day, it had a huge initial budget of more than 1 billion dollars.

Six titles made up the legislation -- Title I accounted for most of the authorizations and distributed funds directly to local school districts according to a formula based on the average state expenditures on education and the number of school age children from low income families.

Title II was involved with aid in the development of school libraries and other resource materials. Title III was designed to promote innovative education programs. Title IV authorized grants to states to improve planning, educational data and leadership. Title VI was clearly an attempt to reduce concern among those members of Congress that rejected federal attempts to control local education. This title included a provision that the federal government could not exercise control over curriculum, personnel or instructional materials.

Yet, by providing monies and other "support," the federal government forced its way into areas not considered by the framers of the Constitution. This legislation would not have been possible without a significant change in the political makeup of the Congress. The election of 1964 had changed the complexion of Congress. They were determined to pass major education legislation. The majority of liberal lawmakers carried the day; so much so that some conservatives referred to the bill as the "Railroad Act of 1965." [29]

This "train", as in others powered by the federal government, has now developed a momentum of its own. By the end of the 1970s, the debate over the appropriateness of direct federal aid to education was almost forgotten. The intrusion was acceptable because it had been going on for so long. [30]

The controversy shifted to federal control of education -- the very appropriate fear of those that opposed direct aid. Additional regulations have been attached by Congress to the dollars in support of education -- these provisions are mostly of an "across the board" nature. One school official terms the current situation as "The Federal Takeover" and points out that, "...state and local taxes together still account for more than 90% of the dollar outlay for public schools in the nation. Yet the amount of federal regulation had increased in ways disproportionate to the amount of federal dollars received...(s)lowly, inexorably, and incrementally, the federal government is taking over education. Especially since 1965, the country has moved -- almost every year -- toward a national system of education...By 1980 the phenomenon of "federal takeover" may appear to be an understatement of the problem." [31]

These regulations carry with them problems, such as large increases in costs that do not go to educate but to comply with the reporting functions of the laws; alteration of local priorities and procedures; and vast amounts of new paperwork. [32]

Education is of critical importance to our nation -- and an important function of government.

The issue was (and should have been): should the federal government be involved in the control of education?

All of these developments underscore the nature of federal involvement in any new area -- it represents a "conscious attempt to gain support for federal aid through hitching onto major problems of "crises" of the day." [33]

The above discussion should not be construed as the only involvement by the federal government in education. Higher education was the first area entered into by the federal government. It, too, has been the object of major federal legislation -- beginning with the Higher Education Acts of 1963, 1965, and 1972. These laws have created a new federal role in higher education, based upon, "a pervasive and broadening fiscal and regulatory presence, and a new rationale for federal intervention -- promoting broader educational access and equal opportunity. Major legislative innovations, based one upon another, passed in rapid succession in 1963, 1965 and 1972. (As they did so), fiscal and political barriers to a more expansive federal role were eroded and overcome." [34]

These early programs were the result of the combined efforts of Presidents Kennedy and Johnson. Subsequent Congressional actions have built upon these intrusions to move the federal government from its role of encouragement and assistance into a pervasive regulatory presence.

This is a cursory examination of the federal impact on higher education. It is included only to demonstrate the dynamics of growth in federal law-making. Initially, the government becomes aware of a need and directs tax dollars toward that need -- in the form of loans, then grants. The appropriation of money is followed by broader legislation to clarify its intended uses. Then these policy statements are broadened to enter other peripheral areas to protect the "gains" made in other areas. Finally, with federal money in so many areas, a decision is made to begin regulating its uses -- thereby regulating those that have had the money forced on them to begin with.

It is not a healthy system. No matter that the ultimate goal of this legislation has been to upgrade education -- the results have generally not justified the tremendous cost to the taxpayer. Here, as in the following section on housing, while the impetus began between 1961 and 1968 -- the problems have outlived their sponsors.

Housing

Housing, like education, is another area entered into by the federal government -- timidly at first, then much bolder as time passed.

The first role of the government in housing was similar to that in education -- investigation. The first major appropriation was in 1892 when the national government appropriated $20,000 to investigate slums in cities with 2,000,000 or more people. [35]

The next major expansion of the federal role came during the 1930s -- again because of the economy. Often these programs took the form of loans to reconstruct slum areas. The first major legislation was the National Housing act, enacted in 1934, whose purpose was generally to, "relieve unemployment and to stimulate the release of private credit in the hands of banks and lending institutions for home repairs and construction." [36]

Another offshoot was the creation of the Federal Housing Administration. Another comprehensive housing package was also a New Deal creation -- the United States Housing Act of 1937. This program included both loans and grants to finance new construction.

By the 1940s, the bulk of federal attention to the housing problem was centered on the needs of servicemen and the defense industry. This philosophy continued after the Second World War and the provisions necessary for returning veterans.

Congress also entered into the area of rent control with the Emergency Price Control Act of 1942. (This was followed up later by extensive regulation of rents within the District of Columbia.)

By 1949, the Truman Administration had begun to reach a broader opinion as to the scope of federal involvement in housing. In the Housing Act of 1949, the national housing policy is "that the general welfare and security of the nation require the realization as soon as feasible of the goal of a decent home and a suitable living environment for every American family." [37]

This act also carried with it provisions for slum clearance

and urban redevelopment. In the 1950s, another phenomenon began to develop. The federal government began to divest itself of some of its public housing projects. The recipients were state and local government that had to create local housing authorities to handle the administration of these projets.

Government planners also began to make a case for the concept of community development -- that is, a systematic, planned approach to the problems of the cities. President Kennedy came into office with an interest in the problems of the cities. His efforts to create a department of Urban Affairs and Housing have been noted previously. During his abbreviated term of office, there were some 53 major items dealing with housing, slum clearance, urban transportation and other similar programs.

Among the first of these was the Housing Act of 1961 which had some 42 different areas including "Below Market Rate Rental Housing," Mortgage Insurance for Experimental Housing, an authorization for more public housing, provisions encouraging hospitals in urban areas, public facility loans for mass transportation, open space grants, and additional housing for the elderly, veterans, and the farmer. [38]

When Lyndon Johnson assumed the Presidency, these incursions of the federal government were used to justify even more. One of the first acts of his administrations was the approval of $150 million dollars of guarantees to construct low-cost housing in Latin America. [39]

Two other major laws were the Economic Opportunity Act of 1964 and the Housing Act of 1964. Both of these contained provisions for urban renewal and housing for various groups in need of assistance. The Housing and Urban Development Act of 1965 contained provisions for rent supplements, low-rent public housing, rehabilitation grants in urban Renewal Zones, authorization to study relief efforts for homeowners near airports, more open space and beautification funds, construction of water and sewerage facilities in connection with federally-assisted housing, urban renewal generally, and lease guarantees for certain small business concerns.

In all, there were some 125 major activities regarding housing and urban development.[40]

The recitation of program titles does not adequately describe the impact that this administration had on the fiscal soundness of the nation. Listed below are some of the new expenditures authorized by Congress during the Kennedy-Johnson years:

1961 -- Open Space Land Programs 50,000,000
1961 -- Housing Act (Urban Renewal Title I) 1,975,000,000
1964 -- Rehabilitation Loans 50,000,000
1965 -- Grants for Neighborhood Facilities 50,000,000
1965 -- Grants for Water and Sever Facilities 200,000,000
1965 -- Grants to aid advance acquisition of land 25,000,000
1966 -- Model Cities Program 12,000,000
1966 -- Areawide Development Grants 25,000,000
1968 -- College Housing 10,000,000
1968 -- Fair Housing and Equal Opportunity 2,000,000
1968 -- Homeownership/Rental Housing Assistance 150,000,000
1968 -- Low-rent Public Housing (HUD Act 1968) 100,000,000 [41]

This is by no means a total list. Even more alarming is the rate at which these appropriations climbed. It has been said before -- but it bears repeating:

Once the government enters an area, it is very difficult to curtail its involvement. Once a program is on the books, people begin to depend on its continued existence. The way to remedy this situation is to restrict the involvement of the federal government in areas where it has no constitutional authority. It is imperative that state governments accept their responsibility and exercise leadership in these areas.

Unfortunately, it is often easier to accept the handout from Washington rather than challenge the people to solve their problems locally.

These two areas do more than just demonstrate the intrusive nature of federal programs and their growth potential. Included in this chapter are the seeds of another growing well-intentioned federal program that is serving to undermine a balanced system of federalism -- grants-in-aid.

In education and housing, the federal government began its involvement through its control of the money. These grants-in-aid are accompanied by extensive federal regulation. Needless to say, these programs continue to carry us further away from the proper course outlined by our Constitution.

CHAPTER NINE

CHANGING DYNAMICS: THE CITIES AND GRANTS-IN-AID

Historically, there have been two partners in our system of federalism -- the national government and the states; each with its own duties and powers. Over time, another partner has been added to the system -- local government, that is, counties, cities, and special purpose districts. The addition of this third party to the system has brought about a host of changes.

Initially, the state governments exercised their responsibility to the citizens of their states. The growth of the federal presence in local affairs and the emergence of a local-national partnership has served to reduce state involvement in solving problems within its borders.

Big city mayors have routinely indicated that they spend more time in Washington than in their own state capitals. With the wide range of federal aid available, the trend has been for even more local involvement with the national government -- even small towns are in constant touch with Washington concerning a host of federal programs. This activity accelerated the trend toward more national and less state problem-solving; which has a real impact on the states and our system of government.

By providing federal assistance, the national government has increased its own financial troubles -- and at the same time created significantly more financial problems for local governments. The culprit in this case is not a sinister plot to subvert the will of the states. Instead, it is another well-intentioned federal effort designed to alleviate the needs of the people.

The Background and Development of Federal-Local Relations

In a discussion of growing federal-local relationships, the

113

questions occur: Why did it happen? What factors enabled the national government to become involved in local matters? Why have the states allowed it to happen?

As with other constitutional questions, there is no one answer. The current national policy evolved over a long period of time -- aided by the growing urbanization of the country; accelerated by a desire on behalf of the Congress to stake out more areas of power; and always driven by the desire to right some of the wrongs that made life difficult for some of our citizens.

The most basic change to confront our leaders has been the change from an agrarian to an urban society. The problems caused by urbanization were not addressed in any fashion by the framers of the Constitution.

The rationalization for greater federal involvement in the problems of the cities is that even though cities existed in early America -- their problems did not become acute until recently. Indeed, there is ample evidence to suggest that urban problems would not have been a major concern of government at any level because so few people lived in urban areas. In 1790, for example, less than 5% of the population of the nation lived in cities (New York City was the largest then with a population of 50,000).

With so few urban residents, they initially had very little voice in government. There was a gradual increase in the population of the cities -- spurred on to a great extent by the industrial revolution and the large numbers of immigrants. By the decade of the 1920s, the urban areas contained 56% of the population. (The suburbs also began to experience growth during this time.) By 1960, some 70% of the people lived in urban areas -- and the growth trend has continued. [1]

Yet, even with this large population shift, it was often felt that the cities did not receive their share of attention or the monies needed to solve their growing number of problems. Several reasons were suggested to account for this: a) legal precedent; b) inadequate representation due to the rural orientation of most state governments; and c) the differing sets of values held by rural and urban residents.

114

In law, the custom had long held that the cities were parts of the states and subject to their complete control. This ruling, known as Dillon's Rule, was established in the case of the City of Clinton v. Cedar Rapids and Missouri River Railroad Company, 24 Iowa 455 (1868). The declaration was that municipal corporations owed their origins and powers to the state legislature. (This ruling was ultimately upheld by the United States Supreme Court.) [2]

Inadequate representation in state government was a direct result of the manner by which state legislatures were elected. A great many states had constitutions that apportioned representation according to land size and not on population -- the result was that cities had a disproportionately small share of representation. [3]

Finally, these rural-dominated state governments seem to have had little interest in the problems of the city dwellers. It should come as no surprise that, "the interests and values of country and city are substantially dissimilar..." [4]

The problems of the city-dwellers appeared to be more acute than those of the rural population. The Great Depression did much to highlight these problems. The first to feel the effects of the economic crisis were concentrated in the cities. When their paychecks stopped, they went hungry. (This was contrasted by the self-reliant farmers who still had food -- for the short-term at least.)

The city residents had no resources other than their jobs -- they were more dependent. The most common forms of mass communication in those days were the newspapers. The larger papers with the influential readerships were centered in the big cities. Their initial focus was on the problems right outside their offices. These were urban problems. By the 1950s, these urban problems had received so much attention that they came to be regarded as national problems. The first of these problems to be identified were the "physical blight of the center city; substandard housing; transportation systems; urban education systems; and water and air pollution. These are so-called "pathological patterns of behavior that attend modern life." [5]

With the identification of these problems came the first

attempts to find "national" solutions. First the observation was made that the cities were unable to solve their problems; followed by an assertion that the states were unwilling to assist in the alleviation of these conditions; then came the inevitable conclusion that it would be necessary to "bring the nation's resources to bear on areas of major stress." [6]

As has been mentioned previously, it was during the Kennedy-Johnson era (primarily the Johnson years) that many of these programs began to appear. The result, as labelled by one expert on city-federal relations was that "the national government has been compelled to develop active relations with local governments in order to make the American system operationally functional." [7]

Without disagreeing that the states, as a whole, had not done enough to alleviate the problems of the cities, it is possible to put another interpretation on those events. By developing "active relations" with local government, the national government actually further hindered the operations of the federal system.

To support this statement, there is evidence to suggest that these problems have enabled the national government to exert control over more aspects of our lives. In one instance, it was observed that by its involvement, the Congress "maximized its own role" and maintained control of the development and policy. [8]

Even with all of these pressures, the question must be asked: How did the states allow this to happen? This was not accomplished without some protest by the states. In debates over the Federal Airport Act of 1946, the state governments made it clear that they "strongly supported" the pattern of federal-state relations that had been in effect up until the Roosevelt Administration.   The US Conference of Mayors wanted a continuation of the expanded nature of these relations.

Members of Congress were aware of these differences of opinion -- in the end, "those in favor of direct contact (between the cities and the national government) were successful." [9,10]

With the stake that the national government had in expanded national-local relations (greater powers), is it any wonder that they conferred these new powers on themselves? The Revenue

Sharing Program of 1972 began sending federal dollars directly to all local governments (theoretically with no strings attached). This set in motion even greater reliance on federal dollars to pay for local services. Many times these funds were used to pay for regular operating expenses; sometimes they went to create new local programs. (The elimination of these funds has caused local government to closely examine the benefits of creating new programs at federal behest which must be maintained by the local taxpayers.)

These political victories should not be considered the end of the debate, however. Once the power to deal with these problems entered federal hands, the responsibility for dealing with local problems came with it. As in some other areas, however, the federalization of local problems not only failed to solve the problem -- it created other problems at all levels of government.

The National Solution Creates More Problems

Two consequences of the greater federal role in local problem-solving have been the decreased state activity in the problems of the cities and a lack of adequate authority to deal with these problems.

One serious impact of these actions has been to take one partner with coequal responsibilities -- the states and virtually place that partner on the sidelines; leaving the battle to the local governments and the federal government -- almost alone.

One of the strengths of state government is that its vista is not solely the local vision of city leaders nor is it the distant, bureaucratic vision of the national government. In theory, the insight of the states should be a valuable contribution. Recent local-national developments have restricted this kind of partnership. (Two areas that clearly demonstrate the extent of the non-involvement of the states is in Housing and Human Services and Transportation. In 1983, the federal-local partnership accounted for about 90% of the total expenditures while the states only contributed the remaining 10%.) [11]

Even in their expanded partnership, the local governments

cannot truly enjoy their benefits -- because they are not really partners. The national government has the ability to dictate terms to the various local governments.

In order to receive funding under some of these programs, the local agency must submit to regular Government Accounting Office audits. These GAO audits have been credited with "centralizing control at the expense of local autonomy." [12]

These federal programs have actually resulted in the creation of more local government. Some of these federal programs required the establishment of special units of local government. Between 1952 and 1962, for example, special districts grew by approximately 50%. [13,14]

Not all of these new districts were the result of federal involvement, but any creation of new government is to be closely scrutinized.

New ideas at the federal level often result in increased expenditures not only for the national government but with state and local taxpayers who end up paying part (or all) of the bill. The last major difficulty created by these programs has been the ever-expanding federal budget (and federal budget deficit).

While the budget deficit is theoretically a problem that confronts just the national government, it obviously has an effect on every citizen of our country. It is just not practical to continue to think of the national budget in "Us" and "Them" terms. Every dollar obligated and spent by the national government must be paid not out of a mystical national treasury but out of the wages of every American.

The ultimate irony of federal revenue sharing is that there was no excess revenue to share to begin with. What the federal government accomplished by this program (which was the expected result of a greatly expanded federal role in local affairs) was to borrow billions of dollars -- which in turn made local governments create additional programs and become more dependent on federal dollars. The effect has been to force the average taxpayer to pay for this effort many times over -- in higher federal taxes, in a national debt that will require major sacrifices over the long term, and even higher state and local taxes to meet expenditures of local programs created to satisfy the requirements of the national government.

The growth of spending in this areas has far outstripped the growth in gross national product (or any other rational indicator of the national government's ability to pay). During the early Great Society years, direct federal grants to localities increased by more than 22% per year. This was followed by slightly slower growth (only 11%). The Revenue Sharing Program, passed by Congress during the Nixon Administration, increased spending in this area by 40% per year. (The reduction of many of these programs has brought some of this problem under control.) All of this "shared revenue" had to be borrowed. So, in effect, we are all still paying for it.

Finally, if remedying the problems of the cities is to be used as check on the effectiveness of these "active relations" with the national government, then the basic premise of these programs can be labelled as unsound -- because all of these federal dollars have had little impact on the problems of the cities.

The cities have benefitted from some of the federal programs but the situation in regard to slum clearance, improvement of inner city education, and upgraded housing has not improved -- and a general perception is that the situation has worsened.

The underlying intention for most of these programs is a desire that we have, as individuals and as a nation, to help those in need. The question that must be answered in regard to every federal program is: What level of government is constitutionally empowered to act in this field? The answer lies with the state governments.

Historically, the states have been regarded as the "social laboratories" where experimentation was to be permitted. Different state governments have different relationships with their cities -- these ties need to be encouraged.

There is no way for the national government to divest itself of all responsibility for the conditions of the cities. The method for distributing this help needs to be modified -- the states need to play their proper role in both the implementation and oversight of these programs.

Further, the states, themselves, need to take a more active

role. They have abandoned some of their prerogatives; these can only be recaptured through active participation on the part of the states.

One major aspect of this problem does lie within the federal government. If the states are to continue to have the ability to address the needs of their citizens, they need to be allowed to exercise sufficient control over the actions within their borders. This will require a lessening of federal intrusiveness in many of these areas.

To find solutions to the problems of the cities, the federal government must encourage state-local experimentation and be willing to accept a lesser role. Without some modifications, the freedom to experiment may diminish as time goes by.

CHAPTER TEN

FEDERAL REGULATORY AGENCIES AND THEIR
IMPACT ON FEDERALISM

An often overlooked factor that has contributed to the weakening of our system of government has been the rise of federal regulatory agencies. Many of these agencies are well-known to the public; the Occupational Safety and Health Administration (OSHA), for example. Others, such as the Materials Transportation Bureau and the Federal Grain Inspection Service have never been household words.

Familiar or not, these agencies and their functions have an impact on all our lives. Through their intrusiveness we now live in a more regulated society. Their independence allows them almost free reign when they decide to add additional regulations. Despite their characterization as "regulations," in reality, the actions of these agencies have the force of law. Today, rather than the one law-making body proscribed by the Constitution, we seem to have a second less accountable law-making body: federal agencies.

By the creation of additional agencies, the Congress is able to enter into new fields -- generally without engaging in debate about the legitimacy of these additional grants of power. As is often the case, the powers generally exercised by the state have been the targets for this kind of legislative effort.

The very nature of bureaucracy is to expand -- to continually seek larger appropriations and more staff. The funds to cover these expansions are borne directly by the taxpayer. An even more insidious tax results from the vast number of regulations promulgated by these independent entities. One study indicated that by 1979, the average consumer aid nearly $500.00 more for goods to cover the cost of complying with these government controls. This number has gone up every year since that time.[1]

This "hidden tax" serves to reduce the buying power of those that need it the most. This is another example of the difficulties that arise when the national government attempts to correct problems--another set of problems is created.

The very nature of these agencies makes the problem, itself, difficult to deal with. These agencies are all created by legislation passed by Congress, but once created, they are part of the executive branch of the government. Therefore, they have two sources of support -- their foundation is rooted in law -- so the President can neither abolish them nor radically alter their functions.

This creates a situation where both the legislative and executive branches of our government serve to protect the existence of these agencies.

Another complicating factor is that often the regulatory functions are just a portion of a federal agency. When the Center for the Study of American Business attempted to identify the expenditures and staff involved in federal regulatory activities, it had to admit that its figures were low because three agencies -- the Small Business Administration, the Foreign Agricultural Service (Department of Agriculture) and the Materials Transportation Bureau (Department of Transportation) did not distinguish in their budgets between their regular and regulatory functions. [2]

For the most part, these agencies have an impact on organizations -- businesses and some local governmental authorities. The end result of this regulation, whether direct or indirect, impacts the lives of everyone.

Charges of unfair (and at the very least, thoughtless) business practices have been a justification in the creation of some of these agencies. This understanding can be coupled with the realization that Congress passed the authorizing legislation that created these agencies with a desire to alleviate some of the problems of its citizens.

Yet, it also needs to be noted that these agencies often continue to function (and grow) even if the need has diminished or been eliminated altogether. Because they exist, careful attention must constantly be paid to their activities to ensure that their actions do not set precedents that allow for further expansions of federal government power.

The Beginnings of Growth of Federal Regulation

The first federal entity created that evolved into a regulatory agency is the Army Corps of Engineers. This provision was part of an act approved by the Seventh Congress on March 16, 1802. The Corps of Engineers had regulatory duties conferred upon it in 1899 -- the first applicable statutes were the River and Harbor Act of 1899.

Along the way, several other agencies were created. The first independent agency to exercise regulatory power was the previously mentioned Interstate Commerce Commission created in 1887.

Other early efforts at federal regulation were functions within the Patent Office--part of the Interior Department, created in 1836. This agency had direct foundation in the Constitution. Article One; Section 8 of the Constitution clearly gives Congress the authority to, "Promote the progress of science and useful arts, by securing for limited times to authors and inventors the exclusive right to their respective writings and discoveries." This foundation also applied to the creation of the Copyright Office within the Library of Congress established in 1870.

Two other early agencies with regulatory functions were the Comptroller of the Currency (within the Treasury Department); established in 1863 and the Bureau of Fisheries (within the Interior Department); established in 1871.

The Comptroller of the Currency had some control over the creation of new banks and other specific financial transactions. The ability to control the currency of the nation has constitutional foundation -- further, at that time, the nation was at war and this act had some revenue-generating aspects.

The Bureau of Fisheries was created to empower a commissioner to determine if any "protective, prohibitory, or precautionary measure should be adopted...and to report the same to Congress." This act, too, had some relevance to the maritime powers delegated to the national government in the constitution. It also could be argued that the marine life off of our coasts could be considered a national resource -- as they are not bounded by state lines.

Both of these acts could be construed as both necessary and proper within the constitutional framework.

These five agencies were the only federal agencies that existed in 1900. Budget figures are not available for all of these agencies, but in that year, the Interstate Commerce Commission spent $250,000 and the Patent Office had expenditures of $1,200,000. [3]

It would be safe to say that the activities of these agencies and their budgets were limited at that time.

Between 1900 and 1932, the number, size and scope of these agencies increased significantly. The first one hundred years of our nation saw the creation of only three federal rule-making agencies. By 1900, there were still only six.

By 1932, five more independent agencies had been created as well as another six that were part of existing federal departments. The bulk of these agencies were brought about during President Woodrow Wilson's administration. A look at these new agencies will also demonstrate the broadening powers of the national government.

Technology spurred the creation of the Federal Radio Commission and the Federal Power Commission. The desire to further control the nation's commerce caused the creation of the Federal Reserve System, the Federal Trade Commission and the Tariff Commission. As agencies were created within existing federal departments, the Department of Justice added its Antitrust Division; the Treasury Department added the Bureau of Customs and the Coast Guard (this later moved into the Department of Transportation) and the Agriculture Department added the Commodity Exchange Authority, the Food and Drug Administration and the Foreign Agricultural Service.

Not only did the national government expand its sphere of activities with the creation of these agencies, it also began spending significantly more money for regulatory activities. An incomplete listing of expenditures for these agencies in 1934 showed that the cost of regulating America had grown to more than $23,000,000 and estimates would put this figure even higher. (No information exists for the regulatory expenditures of seven of these agencies.) [4]

Based on conservative estimates, the cost of this additional regulation had increased by more than 1,000 per cent in thirty years time. This is a significant increase. To put this time period in perspective, remember that these were the years of President Theodore Roosevelt's New Nationalism and Woodrow Wilson's "new freedom." There is no debate about the need for some additional regulation. The combination of increased technology and American business growth created a climate that supported regulatory action.

Many of these programs, some aimed at temporary conditions, live on. In the case of our government, when the situations have changed that might call for elimination of a federal department, the Congress has obligingly conferred additional duties on the department so that it will continue to have a reason for being.

The expansion into these areas also prefaced the election of President Franklin D. Roosevelt and his policies of expanding the federal government.

From the time of his election until his death, nine new federal regulatory agencies were created. In the span of thirteen years, the number of regulatory agencies had been increased by over 50%.

In 1933, two agencies were created: the Farm Credit Administration and the Federal Deposit Insurance Corporation. Two more were added in 1934: the Federal Communications Commission (which superceded the Radio Commission) and the Securities and Exchange Commission.

The National Labor Relations Board was created in 1935 and with it came the entry of the federal government into the (non-railroad) workplace.

The Maritime Administration was created in 1936. In 1937, the Agricultural Marketing Agreement Act created agricultural programs for market orders, inspections and other functions. In 1938, the nation began to regulate aviation with the Civil Aeronautics Authority. In 1940, the Fish and Wildlife Service replaced the Bureau of Fisheries with greatly expanded powers and duties. [5]

The Second World War put a temporary halt to the creation of additional regulatory agencies. After the war, however, the process began again. Between 1940 and 1960, the number of regulatory agencies grew to a total of 30 -- with 16 of these classed as independent agencies and the remaining fourteen operated inside existing federal departments. [6]

The newcomers were four independent agencies: the Atomic Energy Commission, the Federal Aviation Agency, the Renegotiations Board and the Small Business Administration. (The Agricultural Research Service also joined them as a component of the Department of Agriculture.)

In this time period, the staggering change was not in the number of agencies, which did not increase significantly from 1932, but in the increased cost of this federal regulation. The budget for these agencies had grown to more than $276,000,000 or just about another 1,000% increase during a thirty year period. [7,8] *

By 1970, the number of federal agencies had grown to 41 with estimated expenses of $866,000,000 (with the expenditures of nine agencies unavailable). [9]

Most of the new agencies created in the 1960s were the result of the Kennedy and Johnson administrations. These programs included the agricultural Stabilization and Conservation Service, the Labor-Management Services Administration, the Equal Employment Opportunity Commission, the Federal Highway Administration, the National Transportation Safety Board and the Federal Railroad Administration. [10] Possibly the greatest single period of growth of federal regulatory agencies -- in terms of intrusiveness -- occurred during the Nixon-Ford years. During these years, the Congress established some 18 new agencies or regulatory

---

* (This does not reflect the expenditures for seven of these agencies where figures were not available – nor does it reflect some $23,000,000 in income from two agencies that collected more than they spent. It is estimated that these figures should offset each other.)

divisions. These included the Environmental Protection Agency, OSHA, the Employment Standards Administration, the Consumer Product Safety Commission, the Drug Enforcement Agency, and the Materials Transportation Bureau. [11]

The administration of President Jimmy Carter added three more to the list. By 1980, the official number of regulatory agencies and division stood at 54 -- with expenditures of over $5 billion. Again, there was almost a 1,000% increase in expenditures -- this time within ten years. [12]

The growth of federal agencies cannot be viewed entirely in terms of dollars spent. Inflation has eroded the value of the dollar but it is certainly an indication of the rate at which they have grown. A second indication of the growth-nature of the federal bureaucracy is reflected in the increased number of staff positions. In 1969, the major regulatory agencies had a combined staff of less than 28,000 people. By 1979, this number had grown to more than 88,000. [13]

During the time period from 1969 to 1979, the nature of the growth in staff also demonstrates the emphasis of the national government. In the area of Consumer Safety and Health, the staff increased by 481% to a total of 33,000 positions. In Job Safety, the increase was 272%. The increase in economic regulation (areas such as finance, industry- specific and general business areas) was a modest 33% up to 24,000 staff positions. [14]

Since the first major regulations were originally invoked under the umbrella of commercial regulation, it is interesting that the greatest increases and the largest numbers of staff were employed in "social" areas. That is, areas much more intrusive (and farther from Constitutional authority) than the original areas of regulation.

This process has been repeated numerous times during the development of our nation. The first entrance into any field, legislative or regulatory, is usually a precursor of further intrusions -- generally in areas not originally targeted for intervention. This highlights the need for careful scrutiny of any new laws -- especially those that create other rule-making bodies.

In federal agencies, the trend is to expand the activities of the agencies. This is often accomplished by entering other fields.

An important aspect of federal regulatory agencies is their ability to make regulations. Of particular interest is the total number of federal regulations supplementing the official laws of the land. An alarming note is that the total number of regulations currently in force is not readily available. Prior to 1936, no effort was made to identify or codify the regulations promulgated by the agencies. Prior to that time, of course, very few agencies established regulations that had the effect of law.

Some of this information is available for recent years, however, and it is instructive. The Federal Register reports the publication of over 70,000 of these documents from 1974 through 1985. There is no accurate count on the exact number of these items that actually involve regulation.

In 1981, the Reagan Administration issued a directive to the Office of Management and Budget that required that agency to act as a clearinghouse for the regulatory activities of the Executive Departments (the independent regulatory boards and commissions were exempted.) OMB identified some 6,500 regulations from the Executive branch during the years 1981 to 1985. [15]

This is a staggering number of new regulations. They take the pattern of Congressional law-making; that is -- once a regulation is approved, subsequent regulations seek to "define" aspects of the initial ruling. In that way, more and more regulations are added and the scope of the agency broadens -- with a corresponding loss of freedom for the individual.

Regulatory Agencies, the Reagan Administration and the Future of Government Regulation

When dealing with areas as complex as the federal bureaucracy, it is often difficult to present an accurate picture.

There is very little concrete information that exists on the effects of the administration of Presidents Reagan, Bush and Clinton and their activities in regard to federal agencies. The information that does exist, however, indicates that this is one area where some progress is being made. On early study stated that, "the uninterrupted expansion in outlays and staffing in the regulatory bureaucracy which characterized the decade of the 1970s came to a virtual standstill in 1981...Such developments are consistent with the administration's goal, stated in its four-part plan for economic recovery, of bringing about regulatory relief to reduce government burdens in the private sector."

A basic belief of those that favor strict construction of the constitution is that the fewer areas that are regulated by government, the better. This was one of the cornerstones of the Reagan Administration.

In discussing the economy and regulatory relief, it is important to understand the connection between the business community and the individual.

The national government has constitutional authority (compounded by years of activity) to engage in the regulation of interstate commerce. Further, national efforts to safeguard the consumer and address environmental concerns are necessary functions of government. But every form of regulation has a cost associated with it -- in reality, there are three costs and all of them are borne by every American.

The first cost is the federal tax dollar that goes to support the regulatory agencies. A second cost is the interest on the national debt - - some of this future burden is the direct result of the implementation of these new agencies. The third cost, which has already been mentioned, is the cost to the consumer of all of these regulations. New taxes imposed on business (and the cost of complying with federal regulations) are not absorbed by those organizations. These costs are passed on directly to the consumer.

Businesses exist to perform two basic functions -- to provide some product or service desired by consumers and to make a profit. Any additional cost imposed on a business (either by paying more for materials or spending more money to comply with regulations) will be passed on to the purchaser. If the cost becomes too high, the business cannot compete with its international competitors and either moves to other countries or simply goes away. We are seeing some of those effects today.

For this reason, we, as individuals need to become interested in the regulations sponsored by our government. Not only do they have the potential to lessen our ability to act -- they also are a form of taxation -- one in which we have little, if any, real representation. We, as citizens, need to take a more active role in determining what areas need to be regulated. Further, we also need to be more active in determining what level of government actually does the regulating.

Expansion of federal agencies has a significant impact on our system of government and the rights of the individual. Further, remedies do exist. We need to become more involved in the aspects of government that effect our lives. Federal regulation, with its size and budgetary resources, has the potential to be one of the most intrusive aspects of our governmental system.

CHAPTER ELEVEN

THE SUPREME COURT AND THE FEDERAL JUDICIARY

From the beginnings of civilization, every society has had some group with the ultimate authority for the dispensation of justice. The first tribes had councils of elders and the Bible recounts the tribunals of early Israel.

There has been a legal system in America from almost the first days of colonization. Our first courts were at the local level. There were colonial courts as well but no national court system. From these early days, the courts of the various colonies (and later states) were allowed to develop in different fashions. These differences reflected the differing needs and desires of the people that they served.

After independence, as the nation grew, other more pronounced differences began to appear. For instance, some western states have Spanish influences in their laws (owing to their early settlement). Louisiana operates under the Napoleonic Code (which was devised by a group of legal scholars called together by Napoleon Bonaparte). The great majority of the states owe most of their legal traditions to the great body of English common law.

When the Founders of our nation began to set up our national government, it was their desire that the citizens of the various states be allowed to operate within their own laws -- free from intervention by the national government. (Remember here the debate during the Constitutional Convention when a proposal to empower the national government to veto state laws was rejected on three separate occasions.)

The Framers were concerned that state actions might weaken the new powers of the national government; and for that reason, the Supreme Court was given the power to uphold the power of our Constitution.

The framers spent very little time on the description of our legal system. Article Three of the Constitution established the

Judicial Department with "one Supreme Court, and in such inferior courts as the Congress may from time to time ordain and establish."

The Constitution further defines judicial power as covering "all cases, in law and equity arising under this Constitution, the laws of the United States,..." and other specifically ennumerated circumstances. From this clause came the power (asserted by the John Marshall court) of the right to determine the constitutionality of national laws.

The Constitution also gives the Supreme Court appellate jurisdiction (the right to review on appeal), "both as to law and fact, with such exceptions, and under such regulations as the Congress shall make." This phrase gives Congress the right to deny appeals of certain issues to the Supreme Court but the Congress has been hesitant to use this power.

Over time, however, the role of the Supreme Court has grown far beyond the role intended by the framers of the Constitution. Today, the Court routinely writes national laws.

In English common law. there is a long-standing principle that you cannot be a judge in your own cause. [1]

Yet that is the situation we face today. In all questions regarding the limit of national powers, the decision rests with the Supreme Court -- and it should come as no surprise that the rulings of the Supreme Court invariably favor increased power at the national level.

It is demonstrable that even when the court rules to strike down additions to national power, additional powers are still often granted. Every opinion is in itself grounds for future legal action -- even opinions that deny new power can, by the acknowledgement of some principle, allow even greater powers to be added later (as was the case in Gitlow v. New York which will be discussed later).

The unacceptable concept is that the framers would create a part of the national government that would have seemingly unchecked authority. It is even more unthinkable that these same framers would have enabled the national government to decide the limits of its own power. Our history and the writings of our first leaders are unanimous in one area -- that the

Constitution (and our federal system of government) was designed to prevent the creation of an all-powerful national government.

From this, it could be inferred that the Supreme Court has the responsibility to uphold the system of federalism -- yet in recent court cases,the Court has gone so far as to indicate that it will not defend future encroachments on state powers (Baker v. South Carolina).

The government of the United States is unique by the very fact that a Supreme Court exists with the power to review national laws. Other nations have national judiciary bodies but these bodies do not have this kind of power.

The Supreme Court is a truly American institution -- with a valuable mission when its powers are exercised within the contexts of federalism. When the court has ventured outside of those limits, it has thrown our federal system out of balance. The pendulum of power has swung to the side of national power.

The Early Days of the Federal Judiciary

Soon after the ratification of the Constitution (but before the ratifications by North Carolina and Rhode Island), the First Congress convened. One of its first acts of business was to begin to flesh out the federal judiciary.

The United States was broken into thirteen districts (with North Carolina and Rhode Island excluded -- but with provisions for Maine and Kentucky that were not then states). Each district was to have a District Court with a resident District Judge. In addition, these courts were to be grouped into three circuits: the eastern, middle and southern. Two sessions of court were to be held each year in these circuits with two Supreme Court justices and the district judges comprising this court.

This act set out when and where these courts were to meet. It empowered these courts to hire clerks and marshals and provided for their oaths of office.

The act also presented the first indication that the actions of the state courts could be reviewed by the federal judiciary. Section 25 of the act allows the Supreme Court to exercise jurisdiction on cases brought up from a state court on writ of error or appeal, if the situation is as follows: "The validity of a statute of the United States, or of authority exercised under a State, must be drawn in question. It must be drawn in question in the ground that it is repugnant to the constitution, treatise of laws of the United States. And the decision of the State Court must be in favor of its validity." [2]

Soon after this law was passed, during the term of Chief Justice John Marshall, the question arose as to the validity of the Supreme Court's right of review. At that point, the Chief Justice answered, "In the argument the court has been admonished of the jealousy with which the States of the Union view the revising power entrusted by the constitution and laws to this tribunal. To observations of this character the answer uniformly has been that the course of the judicial department is marked out by law. We must tread the direct and narrow path prescribed for us. As this court has never grasped at ungranted jurisdiction, so it never will, we trust shrink from that which is conferred upon it." [3]

Chief Justice Marshall's statement notwithstanding, it is very obvious that the right to review cases coming from the state courts was not part of the Constitution -- it was added by statute at the first conceivable opportunity in the new national government. If this had been an obvious intention of those that framed our constitution, surely there would have been no need to state it again here -- within this legislation. (By comparison, Congress saw no need to indicate that justices had life appointments within this act).

Obviously, then, the first approved intrusion of the United States Federal Court system into the judicial processes of the states was sanctioned by the new national government and did not rely on the direct intentions of the Constitution.

So, very early in the history of our Constitutional government, (run according to the Federalist principles of Alexander Hamilton and others), we have the federal judiciary involved with the state court system -- and indirectly with state laws.

The next obvious step would be to give the federal judiciary the right of approval for all state laws (whether or not the questions came through the state courts). Oddly enough, after receiving this initial power, the national government made few attempts to expand its influence in this area.

Perhaps the continual growth of the nation, its external conflicts, and the growing threat of civil war stayed their hands in some ways. For whatever the reasons, the role of the federal judiciary in the operations of the states was minimal until the early years of the Twentieth Century.

The change was dramatic and it was the result of the changing interpretation of the Fourteenth Amendment.

The Fourteenth Amendment Again

As will be recalled from Chapter Six, the Fourteenth Amendment was an essential part of putting our nation back together after the horror of Civil War. The Fourteenth Amendment was crafted to prevent abuses of black citizens by the governments of various southern states.

As will also be remembered, the original interpretation of this statute by the Untied States Supreme Court served to prevent the states from acting in various social areas -- such as regulating working conditions and other like activities. This amendment originally created a neutral zone between the powers of the states and the powers that could be exercised by the federal government.

The recitation of the activities of the federal government beginning at the turn of the century demonstrated that the national government began to fill this void by an increasing number of laws aimed at areas not predicated directly on the Constitution. This all occurred with minimal interference by the federal judiciary.

If the national powers were to be allowed to expand to fill this void, what was to happen to the powers of the states? Would an effort be made to protect the status quo - to allow them to maintain the control over conditions within their states? The answer unfortunately was "no."

Through actions of the United States Supreme Court, the autonomy of the states has been whittled away.

In many people's opinion, state constitutions often contain more specific guarantees of personal liberty than the national constitution. (Admittedly, the states have sanctioned some detestable practices in their state constitutions -- but for the most part, these abuses have been eradicated).

Ironically, the Supreme Court had looked to the Fourteenth Amendment for almost sixty years with one interpretation. Then, for reasons that have not been adequately explained, they reversed themselves and -- by decree -- began eliminating the rights of the states (and sanctioning greater national control of every aspect of our lives).

To accomplish this, the Supreme Court first began to place the rights guaranteed under the First Amendment under the umbrella of the Fourteenth Amendment.

The first of these landmark cases was Gitlow v. New York (1924). In this case, Gitlow (publisher of a propaganda sheet that advocated the overthrow of American government) had been imprisoned. He sued on the contention that the New York statute that he had been tried under was "repugnant to the due process clause of the Fourteenth Amendment.

The Court upheld his conviction but declared that, "For the present purposes we may and do assume that freedom of speech and of the press -- which are protected by the First Amendment from abridgement by Congress -- are among the fundamental personal rights and "liberties" protected by the due process clause of the Fourteenth Amendment from impairment by the States." Then the Court invalidated one of its previous rulings by stating that, "We do not regard the incidental statement in Prudential Ins. Co. v. Cheek, 259 U.S. 530, 543, that the Fourteenth Amendment imposes no restrictions on the States concerning freedom of speech, as determinable to this question."

Here was the first incursion. From this point, the rulings began to come much faster.

On June 1, 1931, in the case of Near v. Minnesota, the Supreme Court ruled that, "It is no longer open to doubt that the liberty of the press, and of speech, is within the liberty safeguarded by the due process clause of the Fourteenth Amendment from invasion by state action." The first reference cited by the court as supportive of this statement was that of Gitlow v. New York.

This was not a unanimous court decision. A dissenting opinion presented by Mr. Justice Butler addressed the federalism aspects of this ruling, "It gives to freedom of the press a meaning and a scope not heretofore recognized and construes "liberty" in the due process clause of the Fourteenth Amendment to put upon the States a federal restriction that is without precedent.

"Confessedly," he continued, "the Federal Constitution prior to 1868, when the Fourteenth Amendment was adopted, did not protect the right of free speech or freedom of the press against state action...Up to that time the right was safeguarded solely by the constitutions and laws of the States and, it may be added, they operated adequately to protect it."

From this case came another ruling in De Honge v. Oregon that added another portion of the First Amendment, the right of peaceable assembly. First, the Justices began by reciting the inclusion of the rights of freedom of speech and freedom of the press, using the now familiar precedents of Gitlow v. New York and Near v. Minnesota. Then they state that, "The right of peaceable assembly is a right cognate to those of free speech and free press and is equally fundamental...The First Amendment of the Federal Constitution expressly guarantees that right against abridgement by Congress. But explicit mention there does not argue exclusion elsewhere." They close by including this right among those protected by the due process clause of the Fourteenth Amendment.

Finally, with the groundwork laid, the Court takes on the rights of individuals within their states to have some say in their religious matters. The first case where religion was mentioned as being under the Fourteenth Amendment was in Cantwell v. Connecticut in 1939.

A major decision, however, occurred in Everson v. Board of Education (in New Jersey). Here, the Supreme Court adds provisions found nowhere within the Constitution. Within this ruling (which relies on Cantwell v. Connecticut), the Court asserts that, "The meaning and scope of the First Amendment, preventing establishment of religion or prohibiting the free exercise thereof, in the light of its history and the evils it has designed forever to suppress, have been several times elaborated by the decision of this Court prior to the application of the First Amendment to the states by the Fourteenth. The broad meaning given the Amendment by these earlier cases has been accepted by this Court in its decision concerning an individual's religious freedom rendered since the Fourteenth Amendment was interpreted to make the prohibitions of the First applicable to state action abridging religious freedom. There is every reason to give the same application and broad interpretation to the 'establishment of religion' clause."

Here, within a space of twenty-two years, the Supreme Court had included the provisions of the First Amendment under the Fourteenth Amendment.

Making states accountable for the preservation of individuals liberties is not the real issue. All citizens of every state should have those liberties. The problem lies with the additional grants of power that accrued to the national government by the incursions of the Supreme Court. And as in most other cases involving power -- one incursion is merely the beginning. Others quickly followed.

With the provisions of the First Amendment clearly tied into state government, there began a second major assault on the latitude of the states. This took the form of incorporating other provisions of the Bill of Rights under the Fourteenth Amendment.

For years, the Palko test (derived from the Palko v. Connecticut case) had been the official doctrine of the Supreme Court in the oversight provided to laws of the states. This test did not prescribe any specific procedures for the enaction of state laws. Instead, it forbade the states to adopt procedures that would be considered in violation of the standards of justice in the civilized world. [4]

Beginning in the 1930s, with tremendous acceleration during the 1960s, the Supreme Court began to incorporate the balance of the protections granted in the Bill of Rights under the Fourteenth Amendment. In 1968, the Palko Test was revised (by the Supreme Court) to enable them to take greater latitudes in determining what was within the standards of civilized justice. [5]

The end result of this series of events is that the Supreme Court now has enlarged jurisdiction in cases involving the application of both state and local laws. Through habeas corpus petitions[*], federal court judges are enabled to review complaints by those that allege that they are being held contrary to the Constitution -- even if they have violated patently state and local laws. [6]

The impact of this expanded federal scope has been to change the way that crime, criminals and punishment are handled. Remember that the states have the greatest share of the responsibility to protect their citizens through their own legal systems. (For instance, no federal laws exist that make breaking and entering a crime.) Yet the oversight of these laws is now provided by federal judges.

The bottom line result has not been an improved criminal justice system. The general belief is that the situation is much worse now than it ever was. We have a situation today where the rights of the criminal appear to be more important than the ability of society to protect itself.

Some lay the blame for this at the feet of the federal court system.

The damage to our system of federalism may have been even more dramatic. By providing the national government the right to overrule state actions, the national government may now say to the states -- you are no longer equal partners in our system; we are in control.

Obviously, if one partner can tell the other partner what can and cannot be done, the partners are unequal. The question that has faced the states for almost two decades is: How can we maintain what powers we have left?

The Supreme Court has continued its march, however -- and two recent decisions have left the states with very few resources in their fight to maintain some freedoms for their citizens.

Two Recent Decisions

While many actions of the Supreme Court have strengthened

the national government at the expense of the state governments, recently another detrimental effect on federalism has occurred. That is -- in two recent rulings, the Supreme Court has stated that it will specifically not enforce any provisions of the Constitution that would prevent the national government from usurping the powers of the states (specifically the Tenth Amendment).

The first major case occurred in February of 1985 when the Supreme Court decided in Garcia v. San Antonio Metropolitan Transit Authority that "in effect, that if the states 'as states' want protection within the constitutional system they must look to Congress not to the courts." [7]

The rationalization for these actions is that since the members of Congress come from the states, the states must use their influence to keep Congress out of additional areas.

This is truly a major departure from the concept of limited government brought forth by the creators of our system of government. Federalism must have two partners and dual sovereignty (even if one of the partners must be slightly weaker than the other). To state that the Court system will not become involved in the question (on the side of the state, anyway) after having spent the better part of the last sixty years in weakening the ability of the states to respond to these sorts of threats is incredible.

If this were an isolated incident, perhaps it could even be overlooked (in the case of Garcia, it had an impact mainly on the labor aspects of a municipally owned mass transit system).

In April of 1988, in the case of South Carolina v. Baker, the Supreme Court enabled Congress to tax all interest on state and local government bonds, by which the Supreme Court, according to the Wall Street Journal, "finally has completed its long march toward gutting the Constitution's Tenth Amendment of all meaning. The system of federalism stipulated by the Founders has been replaced by what is, in essence, a unitary system of government." [8]

Here, the wording in this case was based on earlier wording in the Garcia case. The Supreme Court indicated that the states would have no shield from this sort of incursion from the Tenth

Amendment, instead, they must rely on protection from federal regulation through the national political process.

This decision leaves the states without any real recourse if the federal government decides to undertake any sort of activity. The Supreme Court's decision to selectively enforce provisions of the Constitution can have potentially grave consequences for the Republic.

Remember that the Tenth Amendment specifically states that the "powers not delegated to the United States by the Constitution, nor prohibited by it to the States, are reserved to the States respectively, or to the people." Before we lose sight of the real reason for the creation of a federalist system, we need to remember that the ultimate master of both of these levels of government is the people. When the Supreme court invalidates the Tenth Amendment, it does more than just cause discomfort for state leaders that desire the power to undertake initiatives for the benefit of their people -- this invalidation also puts all of us at the mercy of the court system and the national government.

Remember that these powers were also reserved "to the people." They belong to us -- now, however, apparently the national government and not the Constitution and the people it was created to serve will hold the vast residue of powers.

The Growth of the Federal Judiciary

Originally, the federal judiciary was relatively small -- the Supreme Court, thirteen district courts and three circuit courts composed of judges and justices serving in the other two court systems.

As the number of states grew, so did the federal judiciary. Other districts were created and more circuits -- the entire establishment grew. This was not unexpected. Indeed, the growth of the federal court establishment has not been as dramatic as other areas of the federal government. This section is not concerned with the number of employees or budgets. Instead, this is a look at the activities of the federal judiciary.

Every ruling by a court becomes part of the body of law. Even decisions not to review laws shape this system. Therefore, it is important to track the dramatic growth in the number of cases presented and the number of cases adjudicated at the federal level.

From 1890 until 1900, the Supreme Court disposed of an average of 455 cases arising from the appellate docket. As a matter of fact, these cases were on a continual decline from a high of 610 in 1890 to a low of 368 in 1900. [9]

The Ten Circuit Courts of Appeals disposed of 1023 cases during the 1900 term. [10]

In 1932, the United States Supreme Court disposed of 906 cases. The Eleven Circuit Courts of Appeals disposed of another 3198 cases. [11-12]

In the 1968 term, the United States Supreme Court disposed of some 3,117 cases; while the combined appeals courts added another 8,264 cases. [13-14]

For the 1985 term, the appeals courts heard cases involving negotiable instruments, condemnation of land, civil rights, labor standards, securities, tax suits, over 1400 lawsuits from prisoners, environmental matters and suits under the Freedom of Information Act. [15]

This is a tremendous jump in legal activity. While the Supreme Court has had modest jumps in the cases that it disposes of, the federal appeals courts had greater than a 300% increase in less than 20 years -- this is in no way attributable to increases in population. All of this can be laid right at the door of an expanding federal judiciary system.

With all of these additional rulings, it could be assumed that the laws were just about interpreted at this point. However, our system does not work that way. There can be no strict interpretation of laws. Every word in every law is open to interpretation. Once the wedges are established, further clarifications are always forthcoming; which create other areas that are themselves open to interpretation.

The law is full of gray areas -- and efforts should be made to eliminate some of this gray. But some questions may be answered by either "yes" or "no" answers. All of this legal activity on the part of the federal courts (with a corresponding rise in activity at the state court level) has not created a more equitable legal system.

The judicial system, like our government, is supposed to serve us. When inequities arise, we have a right to have them addressed by our leaders. Laws should be written clearly and criminals should be punished.

There has been a tremendous amount of attention to the rights of the criminals. Injustices have been done. But there is an equally important principle at stake in our nation -- the right of all Americans to feel safe in their homes. This is perhaps the greatest liberty of all. These needs must be balanced -- for without true justice, there can be no liberty.

Chapter Twelve

Conclusions

Our system of government does not operate in the fashion designed by the framers of our Constitution. Rather than the system of dual sovereignty known as federalism, we instead have an intrusive, bloated federal government spurred on by its own momentum.

The changes that have occurred have not been the responsibility of any one political administration or even one branch of government. This change has been brought about as the result of a series of actions by various Presidents, Congresses and Courts -- all basically built one on top of another.

The States, as political entities and partners in the federal system, must also share some of the blame. After all, if they had been courageous enough to take the steps required to care for the problems within their borders, there would have been less pressure placed on the national government to act in these areas.

There can be no doubt that some of the blame lies with us -- as citizens we have allowed this tremendous growth because the additions of government power always promise to give us something better. But the fact remains that the greatest additional grants of power to the national government have come as a direct result of actions taken by the federal government. It began as an effort to secure enough power to carry out its basic functions and has evolved into the philosophy that the national government may enter into new fields at will. Indeed the vast number of these changes are now institutionalized and therefore basically untouchable. There is no way that we can go back and rewrite history. A great many people now depend on the protections afforded by these regulations -- therefore, it is unlikely that many of them can be eliminated.

There are other areas, however, where the ink is not quite dry and this provides us with perhaps one final opportunity to make the necessary changes.

The election of the Republican majorities in the 1994

elections was a major step in dramatically slowing the rate of growth of the federal government. The 104th Congress did an excellent job of beginning the process. Subsequent budget battles and a weakened House Speaker Newt Gingrich, however, caused a loss of momentum. While the majority of conservatives elected in the Class of '94 remain committed to the ideals that brought them there, there has been some fallout. While much has been accomplished, much remains to be done.

The following recommendations would address some of the key issues:

1) Term limits
2) Tax code
3) Federal bureaucracy and regulations
4) Public-private partnerships
5) Federal programs and block granting
6) Constitutional amendments

Term Limits

There are too many individuals who rely on elected public service as a career. This makes them dependent on reelection and even more dependent on the favor of special interest groups. A return to part-time legislators would be good for the country and to that end legislative terms should be limited.

Tax Code Reformation

Our tax code rewards and punishes the wrong things while encouraging class warfare and empowering a federal tax-collecting bureaucracy. We need to rewrite our tax code to take government out of the business of determining winners and losers. The tax code needs to be simple and fair so that every individual contributes something to the upkeep of their country.

There is no way that the government should determine who makes the "right" amount of money and who makes "too much." Let people make what they can and charge everyone a fair percentage.

Federal Bureaucracy and Regulations

Control of the federal bureaucracy, the 4th Branch of the federal government, is another critical issue. Control will be best established by implementing the following guidelines:

A) Tailor standards to address problems. One size does not fit all. What works in warm, temperate climates might not work in cooler climates. Regulations need to be flexible and tailored.
B) Environmental regulations should be subjected to a cost-benefit analysis before they are implemented. No new regulations should be established unless they pass a cost-benefit test. Is the benefit worth the cost? If not, the regulation should not be adopted.
C) Regulations should have review dates, sunset provisions and should be reviewed periodically to see if they are doing their work--and if not they should either be modified or eliminated. Certain regulations should expire at a predetermined date unless Congress votes to reauthorize them and the President agrees.
D) Some federal agencies should be eliminated. Every federal agency justifies itself by passing regulations it then enforces. Without the bureaucracy, there is no futher regulatory pressure. Cabinet departments such as Education may not be necessary.

Public-private Partnerships

Local school districts buy computers with the aid of local grocery stores. Local recreation departments receive funding from the United Way. Local churches prepare and deliver meals to shut-ins and elderly. Local people know more about what needs to be done than bureaucrats ever will. And local organizations already exist to solve many of the problems that the government works on. Lets work together to pool these resources to find the real problems and solve them.

Federal Programs and Block-Granting

In the past, when the federal government enacted a program, it created regulations and told state and local government to enforce them--sometimes with grants and loans with strings attached. From this point on, the federal government should reduce its involvement in local programs to block grants alone. Send the money back to state and local officials close to the problems and let them use the money where it will do the most good.

To assume that federal bureaucrats better understand how to solve local probelms than the local officals is the height of arrogance. With its dismal track record in solving problems, the federal establishment has nothing to be arrogant about. Send the money back without strings and get out of their way--that is the best approach to federal assistance.

Constitutional Amendments

There are areas where a constitutional amendment might be the answer. Problems such as abortion, school prayer and a balanced federal budget are so broad in nature that they cannot be effectively resolved in the courts. Perhaps a constitutional amendment would take the problem out of the hands of lawyers, judges and politicans and solve it once and for all.

Many people seem to fear the amendment process. Perhaps because they cannot control all of the state governments that would have to ratify them. The special interest groups figured out a long time ago that it was easier to control the national legislators and the national bureaucracy than it is to control fifty separate state governments. This is one of the reasons why they seek consolidated national power. Constitutional amendments not only solve problems (even if we ultimately repeal amendments as was the case with prohibition), they provide an opportunity to put checks on the power of the national government.

A Call to Action

Government (like power) is expansive in nature. It is clear that our own national government (and really government, in general) has been growing since its earliest days -- first because it had to; then because the country was growing; and now -- because it "wants to." This expansion has continued during almost three decades of Presidents pledged to "getting government off of our backs."

The only way that we, as citizens, can regain control of our government is to become more informed concerning its activities. You could say that many new laws mean nothing to you because they do not affect you. But that is not the case. Every new law; every court ruling; every new executive order has the potential to erode a tiny piece of our freedom.

To reassert control, we must begin to care about new laws and court rulings. Members of Congress should be held accountable for laws that add to the budget or add powers to the national government.

State leaders should be challenged to confront local problems using local resources so that the problems cannot become "nationalized," thereby justifying federal intervention. Finally, the citizens of this nation have not been heard from for a while. True, a few citizens participate in the various elections at all levels -- but the voice is becoming muted; the message unclear.

Federalism is not an issue just for scholars -- it is a system placed here for our protection -- embodied in every word and phrase of the greatest document ever to come from the hand of mankind -- our Constitution. It is now over 200 years old -- it has served us well. Now, we must do our duty and begin to repay the service for future generations. If we do not begin to care today, the consequences for future generations may be dire. We owe it our Constitution -- we owe it to ourselves --we owe it to the future of our nation.

Notes

Introduction
No notes

Chapter One: The Foundation of Liberty
No notes

Chapter Two: The Beginnings of American Government
1   Locke Selection, Sterling P. Lamprecht, ed. Charles Scribner's Sons. New York, Chicago, Boston, 1928. P. 62
2   P. 71
3   P. 74
4   P. 75
5   P. 78
6   The Articles of Confederation: An interpreataion of the social-constitutional history of the American Revolution, Merrill Jensen.   The University of Wisconsin Press, Madison, 1963. P. 163
7   P. 163
8   P. 175
9   P. 162

Chapter Three: The Constitution
Source material comes from Notes of the Debates in the Federal Convention of 1787 Reported by James Madison

Chapter Four: The Federalist Era: The Tensions Continue
1   The Federalist Era 1789-1801, John C. Miller, Harper & Brothers Publishers, New York, NY, 1960. P. 65
2   Pp. 109-110
3   Pp. 72-73
4   P. 75
5   P. 71
6   P. 77
7   P. 93

8   P. 94

9   P. 99

10 P. 101

11 Thomas Jefferson: A Biography Volume I, Nathan Schacher, Appleton-Century- Crofts, Inc. New York, NY, 1951. P. 416

12 The Federalist Era, P. 55

13 Thomas Jefferson: A Biography, P. 418

14 P. 418

15 PP. 419-20

16 P. 421

17 The Federalist Era, PP. 58-59

18 Thomas Jefferson: A Biography, P. 421

19 The Federalist Era, P. 57

20 P. 126

21 P. 126

22 P. 231

23 P. 228

24 P. 229

25 P. 230

26 P. 235

27 P. 240

28 P. 242

29 P. 261

30 The Documentary History of the Supreme Court of the United States 1789-1800 Volume 1 Part 2 Commentary on Appointments and Procedings, Maeva Marcus, ed. James R. Perry, ed. et al Columbia University Press, New York, NY, 1985. P. 798.

31 P. 799

32 P. 812

33 Pp. 895-896

34 Story's Life and Letters, Volume I, Reprinted from edition of 1898,   Alan B. Magruder, American Statesmen, Volume 10, AMS Press, Inc. New York, NY, 1972. P. 166.

35 The Documentary History of the Supreme Court of the United States, P. 926.

36 The History of the Supreme Court of the United States, Hampton L. Carson, Lerner Hill Publsihing and Distributing Company, New York, NY, 1971. P. 249.
37 P. 250
38 P. 251
39 P. 252
40 P. 252

Chapter Five: Calhoun, Clay, Webster and Nullification

1   Daniel Webster & Jacksonian Democracy, Sydney Wathaus, The Johns Hopkins University Press, Baltimore and London, 1913. Pp. 12-13.
2   The Papers of Daniel Webster: Speeches and Formal Writings, Volume I 1800-1833, Charles M. Wiltse, ed. Alan R. Berolzheimer, Assistant Editor, University Press of New England, Hanover, NH and London, 1989. P. 284.
3   John C. Calhoun, Nullifier 1829-39, Charles M. Wiltse, The Bobbs-Merrill Company, Inc. Indianapolis, New York, 1949. P. 42.
4   P. 39
5   P. 47
6   P. 48
7   The Papers of Daniel Webster, P. 284
8   P. 285
9   P. 285
10 John C. Calhoun, Nullifier, P. 56
11 P. 55
12 PP. 56-57
13 P. 59
14 P. 64
15 Pp. 55-56
16 The Papers of Daniel Webster, P. 304
17 P. 315
18 P. 329
19 P. 330
20 P. 338
21 P. 344

22 P. 345

23 The Writings & Speeches of Daniel Webster, 18 Volumes, Little, Brown& Co, Boston, 1903. Volume 6, PP. 74-75.

24 John C. Calhoun, Nullifier, P. 86

25 P. 86

26 Pp. 86-87

27 P. 89

28 Pp. 113-14

29 Daniel Webster to James Kent, October 29, 1832. James Kent Papers, Library of Congress, Washington, DC.

30 John C. Calhoun, Nullifier, P. 147

31 P. 148

32 Pp. 149-50

33 P. 151

34 P. 186

35 Pp. 169-170

36 P. 171

37 P. 178

38 P. 179

39 The Life & Times of Henry Clay, Volume 2 of 2, Calvin Cotton, Garland Publishing, Inc. New York & London, 1974. Reprint of 1846 Edition published by AS Barnes, New York. P. 262

40 P. 221

41 Pp. 226-27

42 John C. Calhoun, Nullifier, P. 192

43 P. 195

Chapter Six: The Civil War, The Commerce Clause and the Prelude to the Great Depression

1 Federalism: Key Episodes in the History of the American Federal System, Sandra S. Osborn, Congressional Research Service, The Library of Congress, Washington, DC, 1982.

2 The Power to Govern: Assessing Reform in the United States. Procdings of the Academy of Political Science, Volume 34, 1981. The Evolving Federal System, Daniel

154

J. Elazar, P. 5.

3 The American Constitution: Its Origins and Development, 5th Edition, Alfred H. Kelly and Winfred A. Harbison, WW Norton, New York, NY, 1976. P. 528

4 US Advisory Committee on Intergovernmental Relations. The Condition of Contemporary Federalism: Conflicting Theories and Collapsing Constraints. US Government Printing Office, Washington, DC, 1981. P. 60.

5 The New Nationalism, Norwood Press, Norwood, Mass, 1910. Pp. 35-6.

6 P. 42

7 P. 14

8 Pp. 15-16

9 P. 24

10 P. 31

Chapter Seven: FDR and the Welfare State

1 The American Constitution: Its Origins and Development, P. 528

2 P. 541

3 P. 544

4 Inaugural Addresses of the Presidents of the United States, United States Government Printing Office, Washington, DC, 1965. P. 237

5 P. 237

6 P. 240

7 P. 242

Chapter Eight: The Kennedy-Johnson Era

1 A Thousand Days: John F. Kennedy in the White House, Arthur M. Schlesinger, Jr. Houghton, Mifflin Company, Boston, 1965. P. 630.

2 P. 621

3 Pp. 646-647

4 P. 647

5 Pp. 649-650

6 P. 657

7 P. 628

8 P. 657

9 The Presidency of Lyndon B. Johnson, Vaughn Davis Bornet, University Press of Kansas, Lawrence, KS, 1983. P. 332.

12 P. 241

10 P. 220

11 Pp. 220-221

13 P. 233

14 P. 243

15 P. 250

16 P. 348

17 P. 239

18 P. 331

19 The Federal Government and Higher Education: Federal Policies and Practices, Charles A. Quattlebaum, Government Prinitng Office, Washington, DC 1958, P. 46.

20 P. 53

21 P. 36

22 The Federal Role in the Federal System: The Dynamics of Growth, ACIR, Washington, DC, 1981. P. 25.

23 P. 26

24 P. 27

25 P. 28

26 P. 31

27 P. 31

28 P. 31

29 P. 36

30 P. 61

31 P. 62

32 P. 62

33 P. 62

34 P. 79

35 Evolution of the Role of the Federal Government in Housing and Community Development: A Chronology of Legislative and Selected Executive Actions, 1892-1974, US Government Printing Office, Washington, DC,

1975. P. 1.

36 P. 41

37 P. 45

38 P. 75

39 P. 86

40 P. 97

41 Department of Housing & Urban Development Report, US Government Printing Office, Washington, DC, 1968. Pp. 226-7.

Chapter Nine: Changing Dynamice: The Cities and Grants-in-Aid

1 The Cities and the Federal System, Roscoe C. Martin, Atherton Press, New York, NY, 1965. Pp. 2-3.

2 Pp. 29-30

3 Pp. 48-50

4 P. 6

5 Pp. 14-17

6 P. 75

7 P. 47

8 P. 107

9 P. 98

10 Pp. 98-104

11 Federal-State-Local Fiscal Relations: Report to the President and Congress, Office of State and Local Finance, Department of the Treasury, US Government Printing Office, Washington, DC, 1985. P. 67.

12 P. 159

13 P. 176

14 P. 177

Chapter Ten: Federal Regulatory Agencies and their Impact on Federalism

1 Directry of Federal Regulatory Agencies, 1982 Update, Center for the Study of American Business, Washington University, Ronald J. Penoyer, St. Louis, Mo, 1982. P. 1.

2 P. 33

3　Budget Offices of ICC and Patent & Industry Offices
4　US Bureau of the Budget Report, 1934.
5　Pp. 44-5
6　US Government Budget, 1962.
7　Directory of Federal Regulatory Agenices, P. 3
8　P. 4
9　P. 4
10　P. 5
11　P. 3
12　P. 4
13　P. 1
14　P. 5
15　P. 6
16　P. 7

Chapter Eleven:　The Supreme Court and the Federal Judiciary

1　State Legislatures, "Federalism: The Linchpin of Liberty," A. E. "Dick" Howard, May/June, 1987. P. 28.
2　Records of the First Congress, Judiciary Act, Statute 1, September 24, 1798, P. 86.
3　P. 85
4　Corwin & Peltason's Understanding the Constitution, Seventh Edition, J. W. Peltaason, Dryden Press, Hindsville, IL, 1976, P. 123.
5　P. 123
6　P. 124
7　"Federalism: The Linchpin of Liberty," P. 22
8　The Wall Street Journal, "Federalism's Funeral," April 27, 1988.
9　Annual Report of the Attorney General of the United States. US Government Printing Office, Washington, DC, 1901. P. 3.
10　P. 49
11　Annual Report of the Attorney General of the United States. US Government Printing Office, Washington, DC, 1933. P. 8
12　P. 145

13 Harvard Law Review 278, November, 1969. P. 282

14 Reports of the Proceedings of the Judicial Conference, Annual Report of the Director of the Administrative Office of the United States Courts, 1968. P. 175.
Harvard Law Review 304, November, 1986. P. 308.

15 Reports of the Proceedings of the Judicial Conference, Annual Report of the Director of the Administrative Office of the United States Courts, 1985. P. 248

About the Author

Joseph C. Ellers was born in West Virginia and has lived in South Carolina since 1965. In 1974, at age 15, he founded a political consulting firm and began working in and managing political campaigns. In 1975, he held his first public service job when he headed up the Investigative Council for the City of Clemson, SC. Over two years, this group conducted over 20 studies for the city government on a wide range of issues. While continuing his education, Ellers stayed active in campaign management and also served as the Administrative Aide to State Representative Edward W. Simpson, Jr. in 1976. In 1981, Ellers was selected as the Administrator for the Town of Central, SC where he served for almost three years. He served on the Criminal Justice Advisory Board of Tri-County Technical College in Pendleton, SC and also as the Public Information Officer of the Pickens County Emergency Preparedness Agency for Pickens County in the mid-1980s. In 1990, Ellers was elected to the Pickens County Council. He served until 1998--as Chairman from 1993-96 and as Vice Chairman from 1997-98. Professionally, he is the Director of Palmetto Associates--a management consulting firm in Clemson, SC--a position he has held since 1985. Ellers is a graduate of Central Wesleyan College (now Southern Wesleyan University) in Central, SC where he received a BS Degree in Human Resource Management. In 1995, he received a Doctor of Humane Letters Degree from the Technical University of Kutaisi in the Country of Georgia for his work with their economy and in 1996 he was elected to the Academy of Quality Problems in Moscow, Russia. Ellers has written three books: <u>Getting to Know Clemson University...</u> (1987<u>) Market-Driven Manufacturing</u> (1990) with F. Paul Clipp <u>Strom Thurmond: The Public Man </u>(1993) He has also written numerous articles for professional publications such as Tradeshow Week, the PT Distributor and Quality Digest. He has also written columns for several newspapers including The Messenger and Creative Loafing.